Praise for *Your Portable Empire*

"In a sea of snake oil and get-rich-quick nonsense about fast money on the Internet from people who haven't really done it, O'Bryan's book is a ship of sanity to an island of commonsense e-commerce. This works."

—Mark Joyner, *Wall Street Journal*
best-selling author of
Simple•ology

"The Internet has leveled the playing field, making it possible for anybody to start a business. O'Bryan, however, has given us the easy-to-follow instruction manual on how to first discover your niche and then build it into a big enterprise that can run itself from almost anywhere—all from his successful and proven formulas. A great book for anybody serious about a better quality of life."

—Joseph Sugarman, Chairman,
BluBlocker Corporation

"This amazing book can free all working people to make money doing what they truly love!"

—Dr. Joe Vitale, author of *The
Attractor Factor* and *Zero Limits*

"I know O'Bryan as a friend and colleague. He has painstakingly put together a book, with no frills or fanfare, that straight-up shares his hard-won wisdom. May I urge you to get it and read it? Not only will you enjoy it—but once you act on what you learn, you can profit mightily as well. Why? Because what's in this book lets you stop making the victim's compromise on a daily basis—and start doing the victory dance, whenever you want!"

—David Garfinkel, author of
*Advertising Headlines That Make
You Rich*

"O'Bryan lives the portable empire, running his business from a laptop with a cigar and a glass of fine wine. There is no one better to be your guide as you create your own, because he's laid out every step for you in his inspiring and easy-to-read book. There is no need to be chained to a desk or locked in a cubicle, and your business can take you far beyond your kitchen table with the blueprint O'Bryan shares from his own successful journey."

—Craig Perrine,
www.maverickmarketer.com

"Freedom—O'Bryan's new book makes you understand exactly how to obtain it and create the lifestyle of your dreams. Anyone who can go from being a dead-broke musician living in a mobile home to generating six figures in a single month is worth reading."

—Bill Hibbler, coauthor of
*Meet and Grow Rich: How to
Create and Operate Your Own
"Mastermind" Group for Health,
Wealth, and More*

YOUR PORTABLE EMPIRE

How to Make Money Anywhere While Doing What You Love

PAT O'BRYAN

John Wiley & Sons, Inc.

Published by John Wiley & Sons, Inc., Hoboken, New Jersey.
Published simultaneously in Canada.

Wiley Bicentennial Logo: Richard J. Pacifico

For general information on our other products and services or for technical support, please contact our Customer Care Department within the United States at (800) 762-2974, outside the United States at (317) 572-3993 or fax (317) 572-4002.

Wiley also publishes its books in a variety of electronic formats. Some content that appears in print may not be available in electronic books. For more information about Wiley products, visit our web site at www.wiley.com.

Library of Congress Cataloging-in-Publication Data:

O'Bryan, Pat, 1955–
    Your portable empire : how to make money anywhere while doing what you love / Pat O'Bryan.
        p. cm.
    Published simultaneously in Canada.
    Includes bibliographical references.
    ISBN 978-0-470-13507-5 (cloth : alk. paper)
    1. Internet marketing. 2. Electronic commerce. 3. New business enterprises. 4. Self-actualization (Psychology). I. Title.
    HF5415.1265.O23   2007
    658.8'72—dc22   2007013700

Printed in the United States of America.

10 9 8 7 6 5 4

To Betsy and Patrick

Question: *What's the difference between a musician and a large pepperoni pizza?*

Answer: *A pepperoni pizza can feed a family of four.*

Question for a guitar player who just won the lottery: *What will you do now?*

Answer: *Aw, probably just play gigs till the money runs out.*

CONTENTS

PART TWO   Mind-Set of Success

ABOUT THE AUTHOR

Pat O'Bryan is President of Practical Metaphysics, Inc., an online marketing and consulting firm, and Director of the Milagro Research Institute. He is the author of several Internet marketing books, and has helped hundreds of new entrepreneurs realize their dreams through his Your Portable Empire™ University and UnSeminar training events. An award-winning songwriter and recording artist, Pat has quickly become known not just for his own rapid success, but for his ability to help others achieve similar results. Learn more at www.patobryan.com.

FOREWORD

The Most Dangerous Book

You're holding the most dangerous book ever written.

Dangerous because it shows you how to break free.

Dangerous because companies may try to ban it.

Dangerous because it's the manual that gets you out of jail and into your own life—a life of freedom where you do what you want, when you want, wherever you want—all while making a good living from wherever you park your seat.

This is not an exaggeration. It's the truth. If you're working for someone else, he or she may not want to see you reading this book.

Why?

Because this book is a manual on how to skip surviving and morph into thriving.

I've seen Pat O'Bryan, the author of this colorful "get out of jail free" book, go from his own makeshift prison to the freedom he now experiences.

He was once a struggling musician. He toured Europe and has several music CDs out. He was a talented and hardworking guitar slinger.

But he was starving.

And unhappy.

He was working for record labels and concert promoters.

He wanted freedom.

He wanted wealth.

He wanted to name his own terms in his own life.

I saw him learn Internet marketing, carve his own niche, create his own products, and go from zero to 60 in under a year. He now has his own following, his own product line, his own university, his own online membership club, his own nonstop residual income, and more.

He still plays music—sometimes—but when he chooses.

You can do this, too. The formula is here. The method is here. The ideas, tips, techniques, inspiration, and information are here.

All you have to do is read this book and apply what it teaches.

It may be dangerous to your boss, but it may also be your road map to prosperity.

Read, act, and prosper.

Go for it!

　　　　　　　　　　　—Dr. Joe Vitale
　　　　　　　　　　　Author of *The Attractor Factor* and *The Key*
　　　　　　　　　　　www.mrfire.com

PREFACE

The Most Dangerous Book Ever Written

Welcome to *Your Portable Empire*, the book. It's for you. This book will give you the tools you need to build your own Portable Empire.

What's a Portable Empire? *Your Portable Empire* is a system for creating an online business you can run from home, or anywhere else. It's almost totally automated. You choose your niche, gather your list, build relationships, and solve problems. Then you sell the solutions to your list.

Most people make active income. They work once, they get paid once. The *Portable Empire* system is based on passive income. You work once, and get paid over and over again.

As I made my transition from "broke blues guitar player," to "rich Internet marketer," a lot of people asked me how I did it. Initially, I had no idea.

Eventually, through working with clients in seminars and online coaching forums, a system emerged that can be duplicated and used by anyone to create a profitable online business from just about anywhere.

This book will teach you that system.

Your Portable Empire starts with an idea. Your idea.

This book shows you how to recognize the value of your ideas, and teaches you to package and market those ideas.

You learn how to create an online presence that, with little or no further effort on your part, allows others to trade their money for your information.

In the chapter on list building, you learn how to attract and nurture your customers. In the chapter on copywriting, you'll be taught by one of the best copywriters in the world how to communicate with them. You see, in the chapter on product creation, how every problem is a product.

The trick is to find a problem that a lot of people have, solve it, and sell them the solution. Then, you automatically direct people who have that problem to your solution. While you sleep, or swim, or play with your children, or write your book, or . . . the point is that you live your life, however you want that to look. The money appears automatically.

Then do it again, until your passive income allows you to live your dreams.

This book teaches you how to do that.

However you define the word "rich," with the information in this book you can become rich. Rich in money. Rich in freedom. Rich in possibilities.

This book gives you the information; how you use it is up to you.

In the past three years, through seminars, coaching and producing DVDs and audios—and with a whole lot of help from some very talented people—I've created the Portable Empire system. I use it myself, and I've taught hundreds of people to use it.

I've asked some of these talented people to join us. Each of the "how to" chapters contains an interview with an acknowledged expert in the field.

Don't let the fact that computers are involved in the creation of your Portable Empire scare you. You don't need to be tech-savvy to do this. Some of the most successful online marketers can't even put up a web page. If you can hunt and peck on your computer keyboard and answer e-mail, you're ready.

This is a "how to" book. On the surface, it teaches you how to create your own Portable Empire. You learn how to build a business that you can run from any place you can find Internet access.

- You learn how to build a large list of responsive buyers.
- You learn how to communicate with them.

- You learn how to acquire and create products to sell them.
- You learn how to automate your business so that you can spend your time enjoying your life, while your business continues to pump money into your bank account.

That's on the surface. If that was all this book could do for you, it would still be very valuable. That's good information.

However, this book can teach you "how to" do some pretty extraordinary things that go far beyond just building a business.

My working title for this book was *The Most Dangerous Book Ever Written*. How is this book dangerous? It shifts the balance of power. It puts your destiny in your hands.

Imagine a book that completely reframes the entire management/labor conversation, so that the only people who would take a job would be those who actually loved that job. If a job offered an opportunity for people to grow, thrive, and follow their bliss, then those people would apply for the job.

The people who were applying for jobs just to make money could make money easier with a Portable Empire, and would have no need to take a job they didn't love. Would that be dangerous?

It would certainly do some interesting things to the demand curve. If the number of applicants for unattractive jobs dropped below the number of people needed for those jobs, something would have to be done to make the jobs attractive.

This will be great for the people who want those jobs. It would also be great for the people who can find some higher purpose for their lives than doing a job they don't love. Almost everybody wins.

It was Joseph Campbell who said, "Follow your bliss."

Actually, the whole quote is, "If you follow your bliss, you put yourself on a kind of track that has been there all the while, waiting for you, and the life that you ought to be living is the one that you are living. Wherever you are—if you are following your bliss, you are enjoying that refreshment, that life within you, all the time."

Of course, Joseph Campbell spent the economic depression of the 1930s reading. He found the depression boring. Quite a guy.

Imagine a book that would show you how to make money easily and effortlessly, so that you could take advantage of your brief time on this spinning globe to follow your bliss—wherever it leads.

Just think of the choices—the things you do and don't do—because of money. Now think of the things you will and won't do once money isn't a factor in your decision.

Big difference?

- If you're an artist, the kind of art you make will change significantly for the better if you don't have to keep the market in mind, for example.
- If you're a parent, your parenting choices can reflect what's best for you and your children—and your partner or spouse—instead of what you have to do to make a living.
- I'm a songwriter, and I can sure tell the difference when I'm writing a song for public consumption as opposed to when I'm writing a song because I'm a songwriter and I love to write songs.

Speaking of songs, Johnny Paycheck had one called "Take This Job and Shove It."

Imagine a book that would give you the knowledge you need to never have to work at a job again. Would you sing a verse or two of that song to your boss? Does that make this book dangerous? I hope so.

I first got really interested in Internet marketing when I realized that it was the vehicle I could use to just take the subject of money off the table, when it came to deciding what I was going to do in my life.

For the first 48 years of my life, my decisions were dictated by money. My life was limited by the fact that I didn't have much money, or any way to acquire significant amounts of it.

As musicians go, I was fairly successful. More than 90 percent of the people who call themselves musicians have to do something else to make money. They make music when they can.

I was a full-time musician. I had (and have) a recording contract with a large European label, a music publishing contract, and I could tour in Europe as much as I wanted. I never had a large following in the States, so touring meant flying to Frankfurt, hooking up with my German band, and driving around Europe playing concerts and clubs.

And honestly, the music I was playing wasn't really the music I wanted to play. It was, however, the music people would pay me to play. It was my job.

I also had a home, a beautiful woman to come home to, and children who needed me. They were in Texas, and they weren't leaving.

You can probably see the problem.

The solution presented itself in 2003, when I met Dr. Joe Vitale.

At that time, Joe was one of the most famous Internet marketers on the planet. Since then, he's gone on to become a TV and movie star, and many of his books have become best-sellers.

My friend, Bill Hibbler, a former rocker who was building his internet marketing business, discovered that Joe had moved to our neighborhood. He set up a luncheon meeting with Joe and invited me along. Joe was (and is) a blues guitar fan, and Bill figured that the fact that I'd played with Stevie Ray Vaughan and had hung out with B.B. King and other famous blues guys would give us something to talk about.

Bill wanted to meet Joe to get Internet marketing tips. I was hoping one of them would buy me lunch.

Bill gets credit for suggesting that I trade Joe guitar lessons for marketing lessons. Joe agreed, we made the deal, and my life changed completely. I still owe Joe a lot of guitar lessons, by the way.

Later, over enchiladas and fajitas in a little Mexican restaurant, he asked me, "What do you want out of life?"

I told him, "Joe, I just want to pay my frickin' rent."

That was three years ago.

In the past three years, I've made hundreds of thousands of dollars. Paying the rent is no longer an issue.

More importantly, I've developed a system that allows me to follow my bliss and, at the same time, make all the money I want to make.

This book will teach you that system. If you read this book and do what it teaches, there's a very real possibility that you'll be able to use the information in this book to build your own Portable Empire.

You set your goals. You decide how much is enough.

It's important for you to understand that you don't have to stop doing whatever you're doing to create your Portable Empire. Whether you're working a job, running a business, or running a home—or homeless—if you can find an hour or two a day, and a computer with Internet access, you've got everything you need to succeed.

Imagine yourself free from the job trap. Would that be dangerous?

Imagine a book that can show you how to make money effortlessly and easily, so that you can design a life based on love, bliss, fun, and freedom.

This is that book.

Enjoy.

Pat O'Bryan

www.Patobryan.com

ACKNOWLEDGMENTS

The list of people who have helped shape my life and receive my gratitude would exceed the length of this book. However, this book and my career would not exist without the help of the following people, and I am very grateful to them.

Thank you: Dr. Joe Vitale for your friendship and guidance. I owe you a *lot* of guitar lessons, bro. Betsy Blaydes for your love and belief in me, even when the evidence was to the contrary. Patrick David O'Bryan for giving my life direction and focus. The rest of the Boys Night Out literary and professional club: Bill Hibbler for friendship, inspiration, and answers. Craig Perrine for friendship, inspiration, and giggles. David Pettit for manning the front lines. Rigby Owen Jr., for pulling me out of the fire. Gaea Logan, for the gift of relative sanity and inspired "bopping."

And finally, Joyce and Patrick H. O'Bryan, who are still gliding gracefully through the ballroom of my memory, as Bing Crosby croons "September Song."

> Success is not the key to happiness. Happiness is the key to success. If you love what you are doing, you will be successful.
>
> —Albert Schweitzer

HOW TO
USE THIS BOOK

> Confucius had some fine insights, but also taught that the individual should conform to the norm of accepted moral standards and duties. The only problem with that is that someone has to decide what's normal. And there goes your freedom.
>
> —Willie Nelson

Your Portable Empire, like Julia Cameron's *The Artist's Way*, is a book you do. It's not just a book you read.

In Part One, "How To," there are clear and specific steps to take to build your own Portable Empire. Reading this book, or any other book, won't increase your net worth a bit. Reading this book, and doing it, could make you free from having to worry about money. Ever.

I think you'll find it fun. As each step leads to success, you'll look forward to the next step.

In Part Two, we talk about your "Inner Game." This section of the book is less active. The work here is internal. I've noticed that there are a lot of people who know "how to" do Internet marketing but aren't successful. I've never met anyone who had their inner game together who wasn't successful.

You can find more resources online at www.yourportableempire.com. You can contact me and my staff at portableempire@gmail.com.

PART ONE

HOW TO

YOUR PLAYGROUND—
CHOOSING
YOUR NICHE

> If we listened to our intellect, we'd never have a love affair. We'd never have a friendship. We'd never go into business, because we'd be cynical. Well, that's nonsense. You've got to jump off cliffs and build your wings on the way down.
>
> —Ray Bradbury

We're making this up, you know?

All of it.

Whatever life you're living is the product of your beliefs, conditioning, and imagination. You're choosing it.

If it's not deliriously wonderful, you've got some choices.

You could accept it.

You could blame someone else for it.

You could choose something else.

As far as I can tell, we only get one spin on this mortal coil. One life.

The good news is that we're given a life to live in an infinite universe with infinite possibilities. We're free to visualize our perfect life and then live it. I think we might as well make it fun.

To quote Willie Nelson (*The Tao of Willie*): "If you've made your own hell, then only you have the power to escape it."

STEP ONE IS TO CHOOSE YOUR NICHE

A niche, according to the Merriam Webster online dictionary, is a place, employment, status, or activity for which a person or thing is best fitted, or a specialized market. After you've decided that you want to create your own Portable Empire, your first decision is to choose your niche.

How do you do that?

Fun. That's the big secret. Your niche is your playground.

Later, in the chapter on list building you learn how to gather people onto your playground. It's important to choose one where you'll have lots of fun and can gather other people who will have fun there, too.

Some of my mentoring clients have been agonizing over finding their niche. I think that if you look at it from the point of view of "a place where I can have fun," that becomes a nonproblem.

Once you learn the Portable Empire system, you'll realize an amazing thing: competition doesn't exist. The marketers who are currently selling to your customers and marketing in your niche are your future joint-venture partners, co-writers, and affiliates.

You can sell their products to your list and earn a commission. Your competitors can offer your products to their list.

How can you come up with *your* niche? How do you choose *your* playground?

I think we can sort this out. First you need to chunk the question down and simplify it. You need to find problems to solve.

Right now the problem I'd most like to solve is breast cancer. A very dear friend is battling this demon, and I've lost several loved ones to it. Another problem I'd like solved is political—I'm afraid that Ike was right when he warned us to beware the military-industrial complex. Then there's hunger, homelessness, global warming, and the fact that there's not a real first-class Mexican food restaurant in Wimberley, Texas.

Realistically, I'm not an oncologist, political scientist, social scientist, or first-class Mexican food chef. I need to find problems I can actually solve and hopefully in a niche where I can stay interested.

To me, that's the real danger—finding a niche that's profitable but boring. I think it's important to find a niche you're passionate about.

For example, I'm passionate about self-actualization, and I don't think that's something you can achieve working 40 hours a week at a job you're not passionate about. I think humans were created in God's image, and we weren't intended to spend our brief time on this spinning globe in mind-numbing tedium. I'm convinced that we're living in an infinite universe, and that there are enough resources for everyone. My solution is the Portable Empire concept, which allows you to travel, think, meditate, and grow to your full potential without having to punch a clock.

So when I'm looking for a problem to solve, I limit my search to the niche of Your Portable Empire.

That simplifies the problem, and it also simplifies finding the solution. I promote seminars, create videos, record audios, and write e-books that teach people to create multiple streams of passive income.

You need to find a subject that: (1) you're passionate about, (2) you're knowledgeable in, and (3) is broad enough to have a large customer base.

In my case, I'm passionate about freedom. You need financial freedom to acquire intellectual freedom and freedom of mobility. I'm knowledgeable about the subject. I make a hearty six-figure income doing what I teach. And finally, there are more than enough people interested in the subject to make it profitable for me.

One way to work your way through the niche-finding problem is to take a piece of paper and draw a line down the middle. On one side, write down all the subjects you're knowledgeable about.

A SAMPLE LIST

Raising happy children
Maintaining automobiles
Losing weight
Yoga

Golf

Healthy relationships

Feng shui

Getting a good deal on antiques

Graphic design

Cleaning houses

Cooking

Art (painting, drawing, collecting, etc.)

Music (playing an instrument, writing songs, promoting a band, recording)

Poker

Chess

Investing

Take some time with this. You know a lot more than you think you do.

Then, in the second column, make a similar list of things you're passionate about. PASSIONATE! Not just interested.

Then, see what turns up in both columns. Make another list of just the things that are in both columns, with the most fascinating (to you) subject first, the next most fascinating subject second, and so on.

Now, let's do some research. Starting with the most interesting subject, do a web search to see who is marketing to your future customers. If you turn up just a few results, go to the next one. Just because you're passionate about underwater stamp collecting doesn't mean it's a good business model. Call that a hobby and move on.

If your search turns up page after page of commercial sites—congratulations! You've just identified your future joint-venture partners. You've found your niche.

Let's look at an example. Let's say you're the kind of person who plays 18 holes of golf every morning and another 18 in the evening. You've got zirconium encrusted drivers and a putter that's been blessed by three popes. Your golf cart has a hemi. On the page where you listed the things you're knowledgeable about, I'll bet golf is at the top of the list.

Now, let's also postulate that you've spent a few years reading every book you can get your hands on about golf, have studied with Tiger Woods, and the local golf pro asks you for advice. Your wife would like you to kindly shut up about golf, because that's all you ever talk about.

On the page where you listed the things you're passionate about, golf is at the top of the list there, too.

You turn on your computer, surf over to www.Google.com and do a search on golf.

You discover that there are thousands of people marketing to golfers.

You're in luck.

Your niche is golf.

In later chapters, you'll learn how to monetize this niche. Here's a preview.

First, you need to find out what pressing problems golfers are having and provide them with a solution. You want to identify a problem that really, really hurts them. I live on a golf course, but the last time I played golf, there were windmills in front of the holes, and I was still in junior high school. So I'm going to wing it.

How do you find out what the most critical problem is for golfers today? Do they lose their balls? Do they slice? Do they get tired on hole 17? Hole 3? Is their stance too wide? Are their pants too tight?

Back to Google. Do a search on golf forum. I just did, and there are over 36 million sites that have something to do with golf forum.

Click on a few, and hang out.

Don't post anything. Just lurk.

Read the posts to find out what problems the subscribers are having.

Forums are gold mines. Somebody will post a question. Several other people will join the conversation, mentioning that they've had the same problem. Somebody will post a wrong answer. Discussion ensues.

Gold mine. Home run. Hole in one.

This will work in any niche. They're just waiting for you to sell them the answer. I do this with newbie Internet forums to get product ideas.

Every problem is a product. Find the problem and sell the solution.

YOUR PORTABLE EMPIRE

Choosing a Niche Fun Sheet

THINGS I'M KNOWLEDGEABLE ABOUT

I'm interested in a lot of things. The 10 things I know the most about are:

1. _____

2. _____

3. _____

4. _____

5. _____

6. _____

7. _____

8. _____

9. _____

10. _____

YOUR PORTABLE EMPIRE

Choosing a Niche Fun Sheet

Passion Some people have trouble with this one. Here's a hint. Think of the movies you love, the books you read, the magazines you read, and the web sites you tend to go to most often.

Some drivers have bumper stickers that say, I'd Rather Be Fishing, or I'd Rather Be Surfing. To find your passion, fill in the blank: "I'd rather be _____."

TEN THINGS I'M MOST PASSIONATE ABOUT

1. _____

2. _____

3. _____

4. _____

5. _____

6. _____

7. _____

8. _____

9. _____

10. _____

What's on both pages? Pick the one that excites you and that you're sure you can sustain an interest in. Once you've got a passive income stream established for that niche, you can visit the others if you like.

Congratulations, you've found your playground.

BUILDING YOUR LIST

> I have long been of the opinion that if work were such a splendid thing the rich would have kept more of it for themselves.
>
> —Henry David Thoreau

By now, you've chosen your niche. You're ready to build your playground, and invite others to join you there.

Let's look at how to build a list and to build a relationship with the people on that list.

The dream of every musician is to have a huge concert hall full of people to play to—people who want to hear their song.

I've realized that dream a few times. When you suddenly stop singing and the crowd keeps the tune going. The zing of excitement as the opening chords of your song are played and the crowd starts clapping the minute they recognize the tune.

It feels real good.

There's no feeling quite like it, except, the feeling you get when you build your list of people who are interested in you—your topic, your perspective on the problems associated with that topic, and most importantly, your solutions to that topic.

Then you hit that list with an e-mail offering a product, and thousands and thousands of dollars magically appear in your bank account. It's like waving a wand and making money appear out of thin air.

The trick is to choose your topic/niche carefully and then gather a large group of people onto your list who are interested in your topic.

Every problem is a product. The key is to match the product with the people who have the problem.

That's why you want to target one particular niche and to attract a crowd that is interested in that niche.

Once you've gathered a group of people whom you can contact immediately, and whom you know are interested in your topic, you can rely on them to support you. They're the key to your Portable Empire.

The amount of money they will provide you is a function of the size of your list, the clarity of your communication, and how well you solve their problems.

It's easy. You gather your list onto your autoresponder, where you can e-mail them all at once. This is called broadcasting. We discuss autoresponders in depth in the chapter on automation.

You can also take advantage of the "auto" part of the autoresponder by posting a series of e-mails that can be delivered at predetermined intervals.

Either way, you can communicate with tens or hundreds of thousands of people immediately—some marketers have lists of a million or more— and you already know they're interested because they told you so when they opted into your list.

So you've got a crowd, and they want to hear your song.

Most Internet marketers are of the opinion that their list is their most valuable asset. Why? Because if you've got a list, you can sell solutions. You can trade digital products for money. You've got a Portable Empire.

HOW DO YOU BUILD A LIST?

Once you've determined what niche you want to operate in, you need to discover what the most important and common problems the people in your niche are struggling with.

Search engines are a great resource for this. Just do a search on your topic. Find the online forums where people get together to talk about your topic. Hang out in the forums (this is called "lurking") and see where they're getting stuck.

A little research will turn up a gold mine of problems. Pick the most interesting one and solve it. Once you've got a list, you can just ask your subscribers what they need. But let's assume you're just starting out and want to build a list. Here's a foolproof method.

Do some research online and find a problem that people in your niche are having. Come up with a solution.

If you've chosen a niche that you're an expert in, you probably already know the answer. If you don't know, there are lots of ways to find out.

You could interview an expert. You could go online or to the library and research your niche. Do the work. You're going to be paid well for it.

Once you've found the answer, put it into a form that can be downloaded from the Internet. You learn how to do that in the chapter on product creation.

That's the bait you're going to use to attract subscribers. Put the bait online where your subscribers can download it.

Now, let's give it away! I know. It sounded strange the first time I heard about this concept, too. Trust me.

Once you've used your bait to attract a subscriber, you can sell to them for years and years. Each person who takes your bait and joins your list becomes part of your hungry crowd of people who will buy the solutions you offer in the future.

First, you need to get them onto your list.

You'll use an opt-in form to get the subscriber onto your autoresponder database, and deliver the bait. If you're not familiar with opt-in forms, go to www.Patobryan.com/blog.htm. The opt-in form is the box with spaces labeled Name and Email Address.

We cover opt-in forms in the chapter on automation. It's a form that's generated by your autoresponder software. The form does two things. First, it provides a place for your subscriber to input their name and e-mail address, and puts that information in your autoresponder database. Second, it automatically forwards the subscriber to your "download page," where they can download the bait.

All professional autoresponder programs will help you comply with commercial e-mail laws by adding your address and an opportunity for them to unsubscribe from your list to each e-mail you send. They also work hard to make sure that your e-mails actually get delivered, by working with Internet service providers to make sure they understand that the e-mails sent with their service were requested, and are not spam.

Now, how do we alert the people whose problem we've solved and lead them to the bait?

It's important to remember that in Internet marketing, there is no competition. If you've chosen your niche wisely, you've found other people who are already selling to your future customers.

You probably found some of them when you were doing research on your niche. If not, do a search on your topic, and see who ranks the highest on the search page. These are your future joint-venture partners.

They've got a problem. They've got big lists of people who are interested in your topic. To keep them happy, they need to supply their subscribers with lots of content. That's where you come in. You've got the solution.

Contact these list owners and tell them that you have a great free e-book, audio, or video, which their subscribers are going to love. They can get it free by going to your opt-in page, joining your list, and downloading the free information.

This is an easy sell because it's a triple win.

The list owner wins by building goodwill with his list by directing them to your free content. The subscriber wins because they get great problem solving information for free.

You win big. You get subscribers who are interested in your niche. They have problems and are interested in solutions. They have computers, Internet access, and the skills necessary to download digital products. These subscribers make excellent customers, and a modest group of them can support you for years.

You may have to contact a lot of list owners to find the ones who are willing to give away your bait. Be patient and persistent.

Later on, you'll go back to the same list owners with joint-venture propositions. Remember that you can add every purchaser to your list.

Building a Relationship with Your Subscribers

Once you have some names on your list, your next step is to build your relationship with the people on your list. Notice I didn't say "build a relationship with your list."

You'll be writing to the entire list at the same time, but it's important to write in a way that makes each reader feel that you're writing to them individually.

- You want each subscriber to know, like, and trust you.
- You want them to smile when they see your name in their in-box.
- You want them to come to rely on you, over time, to provide the solutions to their problems. When they think of your niche, you want them to think of you as their expert in that niche.
- You're going to be asking these people for money. You have to earn their trust.

The easiest way to accomplish this is to just be yourself. Write the way you talk, from your own point of view.

Just like in the offline world, not everybody is going to immediately—or ever—resonate with your voice. However, the ones who do respond to you are the ones you want. Writing in your own authentic voice will work much better for you than trying to write like someone else. People know when you're faking it.

That reminds me of a story I heard about B.B. King. When he was young and just getting started, he was influenced by the style of T-Bone Walker (another blues great) so strongly that he was pretty much a T-Bone Walker impersonator.

One night, he was talking to, of all people, a cab driver about the fact that he felt like he could never play as well as T-Bone. The cab driver told him that he was right, he didn't make a very good T-Bone Walker, but he could be the best B.B. King on the planet.

It worked for B.B.

The same concept will work for you. You can be the best you on the planet, and nobody else can do it better. Over time, you'll attract the people who want to hear your information in your voice, from your point of view.

People respond well to a strong identity. Howard Stern, Rush Limbaugh, and Don Imus are great examples, although you may not be quite that extreme. An interesting fact is that their listeners are about evenly divided between people who agree with them and people who don't. They attract huge audiences and huge paychecks because they're interesting and have an easily identifiable persona.

Some online marketers are naturally warm and fuzzy. Others are prickly and confrontational. As long as you're communicating authentically, you'll find your audience.

How Often Should You Hit Your List?

You should send e-mails to your subscribers on a regular basis. They've asked to hear from you by opting into your list. You don't need to apologize for intruding in their in-box, because you're not intruding. You were invited.

There are no rules to this, but I've found that you need to communicate with your list at least once a week. If you've got something interesting to tell them, you can e-mail them more often.

Some marketers hit their lists several times a day, every day. This can be risky and may cause people to unsubscribe from your list.

It depends. If the e-mails are genuinely interesting, or promoting something that's truly exciting, your subscribers are going to welcome them.

Once you discover that you can generate income by sending e-mails to your list, you may be tempted to e-mail them constantly. Resist this temptation.

Although the list is composed of individual subscribers, you'll find that it also has a group personality.

- You can burn out your list.
- You can irritate your list.
- You can find yourself the recipient of a flood of "unsubscribe" notices, as people flee your list to get away from irritating emails. Your list is your most valuable asset. Treat it with respect. Don't abuse it.

Content versus Offers

A "content" e-mail is one that just provides information. Your subscribers originally joined your list to get information about your topic. There's an obligation on your part to provide information. They'll be happy to receive your e-mails if they are useful and valuable to them.

An "offer" e-mail is one that asks subscribers to buy. That's part of the deal, too. You're a marketer, and it's accepted that you'll occasionally market.

Again, there are no rules. However, a good strategy is to keep your ratio of content to offers at about three content e-mails for each offer e-mail.

Lists and Blogs

You never know how your e-mail is actually going to look when your subscriber receives it. Different e-mail programs format e-mails differently.

Spam filters can prevent your e-mails from getting through, and the spam filter rules are constantly changing. You never know which seemingly innocent word is going to trigger them.

You may want to use your e-mails to drive traffic to a blog.

What's a blog? It's the common name for "web log." Mine is at www .Patobryan.com/blog.htm.

As you're building your relationship with your subscribers, it's a good idea to let them get to know you. Your blog is an excellent place to do that.

Of course, you'll want to write about your current projects and the products you're promoting. You can do that on your blog without having to worry about spam filters. You can control the formatting and graphics, so that you know that your reader is seeing the information in the way you intend.

When you start working on a project or writing a new e-book, you can keep your readers informed on your progress. This is a great way to build excitement and increase demand for a product. When you finally release the product, all you have to say is "it's ready!" Your readers already know all about it.

You can also involve your subscribers in the development of a project. For example, when I was visualizing my first seminar, I used my blog to ask my readers what they wanted. I asked them to help me design the best seminar imaginable.

They sent in some great ideas, and I used them to create the seminar. When it came time to sell tickets—at $5,000 each—the seminar sold out in just a few hours.

Why? Because the people I was selling it to told me what they wanted to buy, and I provided it.

I've used this technique a lot and highly recommend it. Ask your readers what they need, and then create it and sell it to them. Blogs are the best place to do that.

AUTOMATING
YOUR EMPIRE

> For you to be successful, sacrifices must be made. It's better that they are made by others but failing that, you'll have to make them yourself.
>
> —Rita Mae Brown

I sat down with Bill Hibbler, of www.gigtime.com fame, to discuss what components of *Your Portable Empire* could be automated. Over a couple of cups of gourmet coffee, we decided that almost every step could be automated.

There are many aspects of Internet marketing that are not part of the Portable Empire system. Adwords and adsense are good examples.

I've set up this system to be easy, quick, and consistent. Once you've got your Portable Empire running smoothly, you may decide to explore some of the more advanced marketing strategies. If it's fun for you, go for it.

ADWORDS AND ADSENSE—BUYING TRAFFIC

Some marketers use Google adwords, www.adwords.google.com, to attract customers. This is a "pay per click" system that allows you to bid on keywords that people search on. For example, you might bid on "golf clubs." You would be competing with all the other people who are also bidding on "golf clubs."

Let's say you bid 25 cents and win the bidding war. Google will feature your site when someone searches on "golf clubs," and every time someone clicks on your link, you pay a quarter to Google. The assumption is that the traffic you buy will purchase enough products to at least pay for itself. It's certainly automated.

However, I don't do this, and I don't recommend it. The rules are fluid and change quickly, with no warning. Like Texas weather. The reality is that the traffic you buy may not purchase enough products to pay for itself.

The Portable Empire system of building relationships and attracting targeted traffic through joint ventures will bring you plenty of subscribers, and they won't cost you a dime.

However, if you want to pay to play, I recommend that you read *The Adsense Code* by Joel Comm, and do intensive research before you start.

Autoresponders

An autoresponder is an online software program that contains the database of all of your subscribers. This is the program you'll use to communicate with them. The "auto" part of the autoresponder is the function that allows you to store a series of e-mails online and to have them delivered at predetermined intervals. You can also "broadcast" an e-mail to your entire list.

I use an online autoresponder/shopping cart service called 1shoppingcart. I recommend it. Go to http://www.yourportableempire.com/tools.htm. You'll see a banner ad for 1shoppingcart. When you're ready to start putting together your Portable Empire, click on that banner ad. They offer a "test drive," so that you can play with it and learn how it works before you commit. They've got great instructional videos that will show you everything you need to know.

You can use 1shoppingcart to create an opt-in form, which your subscriber uses to join your list. The form has a place for "name," "email address," and any other information you need from your subscriber. Usually, name and e-mail address is plenty.

The software at 1shoppingcart creates the form automatically. You just cut and paste it into your web site. When the subscriber fills out the form and clicks "submit," their information is immediately and automatically entered into your online database.

I have lots of lists, divided up into interests. I know who bought what, what state and country they live in, and how long they've been on each list. With 1shoppingcart, I can sort each list separately, or all together.

Once you've got names on your list, you can send an e-mail to everybody on the list with the click of a single button.

There are other autoresponder services, but 1shoppingcart does things that the others don't do. For example, you can set it so that when someone buys a product from you, they're automatically subscribed to a list.

Affiliate Programs

Affiliates are other marketers who sell your products. You can automate a lot of your affiliate program.

You can track affiliate sales easily, because all affiliate programs generate unique links for each affiliate, which encourages their customers to click on their affiliate link, which automatically sends the customer to your sales page.

The affiliate link also plants a cookie on the customer's computer, so that they can be identified by your sales software. That's how the affiliate gets credit for the sale.

Clickbank has a built-in affiliate program that is so automated that it doesn't require any input from you at all. Clickbank generates the affiliate links, tracks the sales, and sends the commission check to the affiliate. Any registered clickbank affiliate can sell any clickbank product.

1shoppingcart has an automated affiliate program, which handles everything except actually paying the affiliate. It will generate html script that you can cut and paste into your web page, which allows affiliates to sign up and get their affiliate links and other resources.

When an affiliate makes a sale with their 1shoppingcart affiliate link, 1shoppingcart keeps track of their sales and how much you owe each affiliate.

Merchant Accounts

Most beginning marketers use Clickbank and Paypal to make credit card sales. At some point, you'll want a merchant account.

Your merchant account will work with your 1shoppingcart account and allow you to make credit card sales. When the customer clicks your "buy now" button, their financial information is transferred to your merchant account, which confirms that their card is good. Almost immediately, the customer is transferred back to 1shoppingcart, and their money is deposited into your merchant account. A good merchant account will deposit your sales directly into your bank account daily.

INTERVIEW WITH "MAVERICK MARKETER," CRAIG PERRINE

> An entrepreneur can become moderately successful doing the same thing that everyone else does. But if you want to be wildly successful, you have to do what no one else has done.
>
> —Tim Gill

Craig Perrine is the maverick marketer and the go-to guy in the Internet marketing business for building lists and doing relationship marketing with your lists. Craig has spoken at almost all of the major Internet marketing seminars, including three of mine.

He's the guy your heroes call when they need help, and he's here to help us.

I met with Craig Perrine at his very comfortable house in North Austin to discuss list building and marketing. We went a lot deeper than we had planned, and we basically ended up recording a complete list-building course over the course of a couple of hours.

You can find Craig at www.maverickmarketer.com

PAT: Okay. Think back. Let's start at the very beginning. This should be very easy for you because you knew me when I knew nothing. When I first started with the mastermind group, I didn't know what an autoresponder was. I knew that a list might be a good thing to have, because that's where your gold is, but I had no clue how to build one.

You're one of the people who has helped me build a fairly respectable-sized list.

Let's go back in time. Let's say I walk in and say, "Craig, I want to build a list. I know nothing. Start me off—help me build a list."

CRAIG: Well, I think one of the things you've done that's good is identify who you are and where you stand in your niche. In your case, the portable empire—I think—is something that existed in your mind and your actions before you named it—in terms of driving around and traveling and having your business and having that vision.

And that's an important part because I think in terms of building your list, I think you're really building a relationship that ends up being with one person. We call it a list, but it really is with that collective one person, and you are going to succeed or fail depending on how that relationship goes. Just like any other relationship in your life, whether it's a friend, teacher, spouse, co-worker—it doesn't really matter, a lot of the same principles apply.

So in some ways, you already know everything you need to know if you're successful in those areas. It's just a question of how do you project who you are out to your subscribers so that they feel like they know who you are, they like you, and that they also trust you enough with their money to buy from you.

The ultimate end for an information publisher, or in any business, is to make money. In the way that I teach doing it, you end up making money by serving your subscriber.

You've done that, Pat, by identifying what your target market wanted, and you've created a series of products and experiences for them, and you've told them candidly about your journey along the way.

You've got your blog, you've done joint ventures with people with like-minded lists, and that is a perfect way to build a list—with joint ventures with people who have lists that are already interested in what you have to offer.

I know that the concept of joint ventures can be intimidating to people who don't know anybody.

In your case, you approached Joe Vitale and said, "Hey, this is what I want to do," and that was remarkably successful. You didn't know anybody, either. That's the point I'd like to make to people. I didn't know anybody in this particular niche before 2003.

PAT: And now you're one of the leaders in Internet marketing, and you're speaking at Big Seminar 7.

CRAIG: Yes, in April (2006).

PAT: Before we start talking about how to establish a relationship with our list, let's go back to square one. What should we do before we start attracting?

CRAIG: The first thing you need to do is understand who your target subscriber is. Let's say that you are talking to a group of people who share a common interest. I really think you should consider focusing on that specifically, because the key to getting someone to subscribe to your list is to have something they want. Whether it's something they're curious about, or something that will solve a problem for them, or whether you're going to keep them in the loop about a topic they want be on top of.

Whatever your reason for contacting them by e-mail, you have to know what they want in the first place, or you won't know what to offer them. This is where a lot of folks go wrong—they try to sell what they have to sell. You have to be concerned with whether what you have is even in demand online at all. And if it's not, then your list is going to be a tough thing to build.

If what you have is extremely interesting to a targeted group of people, building a list is really very easy. It's much more easy than you think it is, I'll bet.

PAT: That's good news. And there's a long discussion that we can get into about finding your passion and researching the market.

CRAIG: Don't skip that step. I have several times, and it's painful. It is worth spending at least half an hour on Google searching for words that relate to your niche market and seeing what comes up. If it comes up as a bunch of lonely search results with no ads and nobody selling anything, I think you have to beware.

You can go to eBay and Amazon and see what book titles and products are for sale in those massive marketplaces, and if you don't find anything—beware.

The thing that I want you to do is, yes, find something that you're passionate about. There are a relatively small number of business-people who can, in the abstract, be aware of a market and sell to it without having any kind of personal interest in the topic.

Especially in the "how to" market, it's good to have a deep knowl-edge of your target market by being a part of it.

The challenge of that is that just following your passion can lead you to make some pretty bonehead mistakes. Some niches that you're passionate about are not valid business opportunities, and because you're so passionate about them you may be all too willing to overlook that hard reality.

PAT: You could call those "hobbies."

CRAIG: Yeah, I love hobbies, and some things are more charity oriented. But the fact is that if someone's not currently spending money on what you're trying to sell, do that later when you have capital to burn. Then you can be the pioneer. There's no need to try and rein-vent the wheel. You can just see what's working for other people and innovate. That's a much better way to do things.

PAT: Let's chunk way down. To actually build a list you need to establish an account with an autoresponder company. You use Aweber, I use 1shoppingcart, they both do kind of the same thing.

CRAIG: Let's define what an autoresponder is for folks. It's basically software that allows you to have a list of people and their e-mail ad-dresses, at a minimum. And then, it allows you to send them an au-tomated sequence of e-mails that go out at whatever schedule you determine, so that if you tell it to go out one e-mail every other day, then, every other day your subscribers are going to get your e-mails.

An autoresponder allows you to also send out e-mails in a broad-cast, so that you can just type an e-mail and send it to your entire list. It's not automatic; it doesn't go out without your sending it.

The autoresponder is the software that allows all that to happen. It has the database of the subscribers and the tools to write an e-mail and send it.

How fancy it is, whether it's a service that you pay for or some-thing that you put on your own server, or something that you put on your computer at home—those are choices that you need to make.

I'm just going to say that I use a professional autoresponder company, and they're very conscientious about the whole process of getting your e-mails delivered.

It's kind of a no-brainer service you can use. I'm getting 99 percent of my e-mails delivered. If you use a program on your own computer, there's a chance of getting 50 percent or fewer of your e-mails delivered.

You need to have a place to get your subscribers to opt in. That means they're giving you their name and e-mails voluntarily, and permission to follow up with e-mails to them.

You want to build a list of people who know, like, and trust you.

PAT: I want to get into that—the value of a dedicated, smaller list versus a scattered big list. But let's pay attention to our visual learners here. Do you have an opt-in script at maverickmarketer.com?

CRAIG: Yes. If you go to www.maverickmarketer.com, you'll see that I am actually implementing the process that I recommend that you use. The site isn't fancy, so that should give you some hope—you don't have to have a $50,000 web designer.

I'll give you some interesting statistics. Forty-nine percent of the people who go to that web site decide to enter their name and e-mail address.

PAT: Pretty amazing.

CRAIG: Yes, it's more typical to have much less than that. Of those who decide to put in their name and e-mail address, over 90 percent confirm their subscriptions. If you look at the page, you'll see why. I tell them exactly what to expect when they opt-in. That's an important step. You tell them, "You're going to get an e-mail, right now, from this e-mail address, that's going to ask you to confirm your subscription—and you won't get anything until you do that."

So, you're telling them to expect it now, who it's going to be from, and why it's important. And by doing that, there's no confusion.

And that's important because there are a lot of folks—I used to be one of them—who find this whole Internet marketing thing to be kind of abstract and weird at first, because they're not familiar with it. And with anything you're not familiar with, even the smallest thing can be an obstacle to getting something done because you don't know what to do next.

But I want to give you encouragement that, after a while, especially if you take training like what you're offering, they're going to become familiar with those things, and they're going to seem like no big deal.

It's just that in the beginning, like anything, you want to give people step-by-step instructions so that they get what they want, and you get what you want.

PAT: That's really important in copywriting and general communication—telling your reader what you want them to do and urging them to take action. I think you're absolutely right—even on the opt-in page, which is what we're talking about here, you can't assume. They may be even more of a newbie than you are, and they may not know what's going on behind the scenes. So you tell them that "you're going to get an e-mail to confirm your subscription to the list you just asked to join, and if you really want to join this list, you need to respond."

CRAIG: Right. Just say as much as you need to say to get the point across.

I built that web site in half an hour, right before a teleseminar. The host asked me if I wanted him to send people someplace where they could sign up. I was just starting this concept of maverick marketer at the time, so I just whipped up this site and wrote down my impression of what I was going to offer them, and the e-course you receive when you sign up didn't even exist when I first created it. And it ended up getting created in a couple of days.

It has worked very nicely for months without me doing anything to it, even though it doesn't even really follow all the stuff that I would teach you if you were one of my clients.

The fact is that it works, it's getting a good response, the list is growing, I've made a very nice living on a very part-time basis building that list with interviews and teleseminars. It has pulled in a heck of a response—$10, sometimes $17 per subscriber for every name on the list.

PAT: Per month?

CRAIG: Per promotion.

PAT: Per promotion?!

CRAIG: Yes. I haven't done a promotion every month, but in about four months that site has pulled in about $50,000.

PAT: Wow.

CRAIG: Yes. I just did my stats. And that's on a list of 1,800 people.

PAT: 1,800.

CRAIG: Yes. Without duplicates, I did a $20,000 promotion for a joint-venture product that pulled in 20 sales at $1,000 apiece.

And that was to 1,800 people.

PAT: In the Internet marketing world, a list of 1,800 is tiny.

CRAIG: It really is. I had a list, up until last year, of over 30,000, that I owned jointly with another company. When I decided to go off on my own, I walked away from the rights to mail to that list. So I ended up doing a number of things with consulting, and I've got some great stories to share with you about that.

But the fact is, I was in a position much like you are, perhaps, of having to rebuild my list.

The fact I became intensely aware of was Wow, I've got to start all over again and build a list, and there it was. My first promotion was for a product that cost $1,000. There was some synergy between the product and what I knew my list wanted—I'll talk some more about that in a minute.

But we pulled in 10 sales of $1,000 apiece with a list of 800 subscribers. That's over $10 per subscriber.

Some people boast that they get 50¢ to $1.00 per name on their list, and here I am pulling in over $10 because of the relationship I've built up with these people, and people in the industry.

Again, I want to stress, before 2003 I didn't know any of those people and they didn't know me.

I say that because I know you might be thinking. How does that apply to me?

Don't think that way, because every journey begins with the first step, and if you make assumptions about what you can and cannot do based on where you are right now, even just based on what you're consciously aware of, you're making a huge mistake about what your real potential is, because you don't actually know what can happen once you start on this journey because it's really amazing these days.

Look at you. You are literally the poster child for "I can do anything." You had no money, no marketing experience, and were probably fairly against the business in general before you started. You're a self-described "broke blues guitarist." And I have a number of musician friends, and none of them are as successful monetarily, or have anything to do with business the way you do.

So, if people want to look at a situation that was unlikely on the surface to result in huge exponential growth rates in their business, I'd have to say you are a pretty good candidate. Not because of inherent capability, but based on initial appearances and what you'd assume.

But, the fact is, that's what's possible with this. You can just be yourself, find what people want, serve it to them, and then, you're going to make money and they're going to be happy, and it's going to grow, and all of a sudden your entire life can be different.

And we're talking today about the steps that are involved in doing that. I just want to give you a little pep talk about short-selling yourself, and whether you, personally, can do this or not.

You could be a graduating student, you could be a single mom, you could be someone who got laid off three years ago, you could be anybody—you could even be a blues musician. Maybe you even suck as a blues musician.

You happen to be very talented, but you didn't know anything about laptop computers, and now here we are with your recording studio right here in my office, and we're going to be giving you lessons that literally have taken me years to put together and been worth the lifestyle I have now.

I support my family and wouldn't dream of having a job, we built our dream house this last summer—and that was when I started over from scratch. I walked away from my partnership last year and was faced with owning nothing—I had no product, no rights to anything, no list. All I had was relationships, and that's what I'm talking about today.

PAT: I want to go into the fact that relationships go both ways. Your relationships with other marketers who had existing lists and were able to feed you names, and then your relationships that you've built with your subscribers, which have resulted in an alarmingly loyal list.

CRAIG: I want to say something about that. I really haven't done the one thing, the ace up my sleeve that I haven't pulled yet. And that is the opportunity that I have to do joint ventures with a broad range of people that I've met in the industry.

I haven't actually done that with maverick marketer. My list will grow very quickly when I start doing that. I've been laying the groundwork.

I had relationships where, for example, if someone was launching a book, I would offer my e-course as a bonus. If I did a teleseminar, I would say ,"Go check out maverickmarketer.com."

So, I did have those opportunities. But frequently I was supporting someone else's launch, or was a guest expert, or something like that. I haven't actually done what I was telling you is quite possible, which is to do joint ventures with people.

And I really didn't teach this before because I felt like a lot of people didn't have my network of friends, so it's not really fair for me to say ,"Go do joint ventures." But then I thought about it, and realized that I didn't know these people, either. It's not like I was born with a rolodex in my crib.

I just started going to seminars and started meeting people. I did know my stuff, but I had to learn a lot as I went along. I really think you need to be passionate about your niche and learn what it takes to succeed in that niche: what people want, what they're buying. And if you can either represent somebody else's product to fill that need or create your own, or if you can interview people and create products that way—one way or the other you can start to build that relationship.

I'll give you an example. Now that I'm running my blog and have a bit of a profile in the industry, one of my subscribers wrote to me and said, "Hey, I've got this book," and asked me to promote it. And I'm actually reviewing it right now and I'm probably going to promote it—because I like it.

There are a number of people like me in this industry who want to help. If someone has a product, we'd love to joint-venture and get your name out there. It's not about getting rich quick or suddenly being a rock star—it's just about getting started.

And you'd be surprised at how a few weeks or a few months can really change your life if you just start taking the actions we're talking about today.

So if you study your niche and find the people who are successful in that niche—whether through e-mail, phone, or by going to an event and meeting them in person—you're going to be able to catapult your success.

And do it in the ways we're talking about here today, with your actual relationships that you build, instead of some of the more corny ways that some people talk about.

It's really just about making friends with people, and doing the right thing, and before you know it, you'll have opportunities left and right.

PAT: Let's back up. We go to maverickmarketer.com and we see a box, and it says "name," and "email address." Do you use FrontPage to build your web sites?

CRAIG: FrontPage or DreamWeaver. I am not a web designer. I don't even play one on TV. I just knew how to type. I have no idea about the technical aspects. Just look at maverickmarketer.com—that's homemade, buddy.

PAT: Where I'm going with this is that there are "off the shelf" products that you can use to make web pages. And to get that box onto your web page—the opt-in form—how did you do that?

CRAIG: So much easier than you might think. Two things need to happen there. First of all, when you open up a program like this, like DreamWeaver, let's say you just open a blank document. You put it on a setting like "design view," where you see what it's going to look like. You don't see the html code, you just see what it's going to look like on the web site. You start typing "discover the secrets to raising puppies" or whatever. Type some bullet points about why they might want to subscribe.

And then, you're going to need to know what a table is. So you just click "insert table." And then you're going to have to pick a dimension, and I would suggest that your overall width of your web site be about 640 pixels wide.

Now, take all this with a grain of salt, because I'm not a web designer. I'm just going to tell you want I do in about twenty minutes to put up a web site that will work.

There's this table that's 640 pixels wide. Where you want the opt-in box, like I did with maverick marketer, you're going to have a bunch of text going down the page. When that ends, add a space or two, and insert this new table—and you might make it like 440 pixels, so it's less wide.

Then you go to your autoresponder account, and they'll walk you through the steps of creating a subscriber form. What you'll do is say, "Okay I'm going to create this e-mail series called maverick marketer main list." Put in your name and return address—and by the way, with Aweber and 1shoppingcart there are videos that show you exactly how to do this right on the site.

Then it's going to create the web form to capture the name and e-mail address. You can capture more things if you want to: street address, and so on. You can ask for anything—Social Security number—but you're not going to get it.

That's why I just ask for first name and e-mail address. I want to be able to customize the name on the e-mails. If you ask them for too much information, they won't opt in.

You ask for those two things in your web form, and Aweber or 1shoppingcart will automatically generate the web code, that you literally cut and paste into FrontPage or DreamWeaver—put it in that second table.

There's one little trick here. You have to switch from design view to html code view to paste in the code.

PAT: In FrontPage that's just a little tab.

CRAIG: It's real simple. It's the same way in DreamWeaver. Just a little button you click.

Then you switch it back to design view and you'll see the form. That's really it.

If that sounds confusing, it doesn't matter. It doesn't mean you can't do it. Go ahead and log into an account at 1shoppingcart or Aweber, and they'll have clear instructions on how to do that.

And you don't even have to learn all this web site stuff. There are services like www.elance.com and www.rentacoder.com that will do it for you cheaply.

It looks fancy, but it's no big deal.

PAT: Well, you can go to elance, there's lots of places to get this done—but this is the one technical skill that I think is important for someone who's really building their Portable Empire to actually get.

Because a lot of times, you'll have an idea, and 30 minutes later, it's a web page that people can look at. If they like your idea, they'll give you their information—and maybe even give you their money.

CRAIG: A great thing to do that I've seen some people do quite successfully is to partner. There are a lot of folks out there who understand how to make web sites—they're technical—and things that you find intimidating, they can do easily. But they don't know a darn thing about marketing, and they find the marketing intimidating.

So just figure out which person you are. If you're really good at the technical stuff, but you find the idea of copywriting to be something that's going to make you uncomfortable, then, you be the tech person and let someone else do the marketing—which is what I am. I'm a marketing person.

I don't really have the ability to do products or web design. I admire it in others, but I don't really feel that comfortable with it. So I partner with people who can do that stuff, and that's great, because then everybody's happy.

There's a number of different ways to skin this cat—but what you're saying, which I agree with, is that you should understand this. You should learn to make a web page, you should learn copywriting.

You may never master it all, but two things will happen. One, it will go into your brain on a subconscious level and you'll get comfortable with it, and two, you'll know how to work with people and know when they're doing a good job.

PAT: This is all true. These are all great options. And I'm just going to be a little bit of a contrarian here, because they've made it so easy. If you can open Microsoft Word and type a letter, you're 99 percent of the way there to having all the skills you need to put up a simple web site, go over to Aweber or 1shoppingcart and cut and paste the script that they automatically make for you back into your page, put it online, and for most promotions—that's good enough.

In my office, if we're doing a big promotion, we'll hire a real web designer and a graphics pro, and the page will look like a million bucks.

But there are a lot of promotions I do—especially if I'm giving something away—where, really, the cosmetics of the page are irrelevant. And to be able to do that yourself, especially since the tools are right there—they're not expensive, and they're alarmingly easy—I really recommend that if you're going to be self-sufficient, go ahead and learn it.

CRAIG: Yes. It's not very hard. If you think this is going to stop you, and you're going to quit over it—don't quit. Find some other way around it.

But actually, I've done what you suggested. I know how to do things so that I'm happy with it. I'm having someone develop graphics for me, because I have no concept of how to do that, but I'm comfortable with what I've done.

That maverickmarketer.com is coming up on its one-year anniversary now, it's done really, really well, and I did that in about half an hour.

People have opted in there and become subscribers in spite of the design of the web site. I don't know that that web site sold anybody on anything—but I'm not trying to. I'm trying to get people to sign up for the e-course and get to know me.

PAT: Well, let's go there. That's the next place to go. To attract people onto your list, you're giving away a free course. Is that a good idea?

CRAIG: There are a number of reasons why I've done it the way I've done it. The main thing is—you have something they want. Hopefully, from some burning place inside them, they want what you have. If you don't have that, you're not going to build a list quickly and easily, and the people you get on your list will be confused and not sure why they're there.

You need to have something they want.

In my case, I happen to know a lot of people are uncomfortable with "hypey" marketing. They don't know how to stand out so that people notice them and their offer. So I decided to start maverick marketer to solve that problem. That's what I had done. I'd found from the feedback that I've gotten as an e-mail marketer that people really bonded with me, so I figured that my unique selling proposition is that I'm going to teach people how to draw out who they are so they can stand out by just being real and offering value.

So much of what's online today is complete nonsense or hype or impersonal or unbelievable. Simply by being yourself and having something genuine to offer will make you stand out a lot faster than any amount of screaming or jumping up and down that you could do.

So that's what maverick marketer is all about: being independent in your approach to marketing, being true to yourself. You just have to be yourself.

And find people who identify with you. Folks who identify with you, or me, or our friend Joe Vitale, identify with us because they do.

If you have someone who likes you and wants to do business with you, they're going to be loyal. If they don't like you, they probably won't be on your list. So you can do a lot with a small number of people if they feel that "this person is just like me—we're on the same path. I'm learning what I need to and I'm resonating with their ethics and how they go about things."

Which is a big deal in this business, because a lot of people are concerned about getting ripped off. Not only in the making money field, but on the Internet in general.

So being yourself, a real, three-dimensional person, is going to make you stand out in their life. And you can be a real mentor to people without really working too hard.

So maverick marketer is solving a problem. It's not exactly an entry level problem for some people, but it's my little thing—what I wanted to do.

I would suggest that if you're starting from scratch, that you pick something more practical and hands on—like, "Here's how you do graphics for a web page."

I talk to people on the level of, "Hey, if you're lost, let me show you what worked for me." And I deliver that in the form of an e-course. The e-course is the bait to sign up for my list. By bait, I mean that I give them a healthy taste of what they want—seven secrets that are a big deal—and I charge clients a lot of money to take them through that same process.

So the e-course gets me a lot of fans because they say, "Wow, I learned more with that than I learned in some courses I've bought."

That's the effect that I want to have, and I can deliver that in an e-course. I could have delivered that in a series of videos or audios. It could have been a free ticket to a teleseminar. It could have been any number of things.

Anything that you can offer for free could be bait. I like the e-course because it tells them that I'm going to follow up with them a number of times. They get used to seeing my name in their in box.

An e-course is the way to start that because you say, "I'm going to give you seven secrets." That's seven excuses to e-mail them.

In that e-course, I'm going to lay the groundwork for continuing to e-mail them. And, of course, I make it very easy for them to un-subscribe if they want to.

In fact, that's the law—and another good reason to use Aweber or 1shoppingcart. They do that automatically in every e-mail.

The e-course is the reason why they're willing to give you their name and e-mail address in the first place.

PAT: Let's recap. It seems like the first step is to decide who you are. Are you going to be the guy who teaches about beanie-baby collecting, or are you going to be the guy who teaches copywriting? That's your first decision.

And then, who do you want on your list? That's an easy one. If you're going to be the copywriting guy, you want people who are passionate about copywriting.

And then, you want to get them on your list. The way to do that—you call it bait, I've heard it called an ethical bribe—is you're trading something of value on the subject that you want to provide information on for their first name and e-mail address. And it's a fair trade because you're giving them something of value.

At that point, their name and their e-mail address goes to this magic database at Aweber or 1shoppingcart.

CRAIG: Right. And here's my purpose. I feel that my purpose as an info-preneur is to be the bridge between where you are and where you want to go. In my industry that happens to be e-mail marketing or relationship marketing. If you have no list, no relationship, nothing, then I want to be the bridge that you can cross to get to where you want to be—to where you have a list, you're making money, you can quit your day job.

It may be a useful concept for any infopreneur. Let's say you know a lot about dog training, or how to get a pilot's license in less than a year, or how to avoid a divorce. Any of the how-to things that you see selling out there—your function really is to bring them from one place to another.

You may not be Donald Trump, I can't teach you how to be a bil-lionaire magnate and own the media—that's not something I've done. But I can teach you how to make multi-six figures online. That's my deal.

I don't run around saying, "Hey, wanna make a hundred thousand dollars a year?" That's not what I teach people as a concept. I teach my skill-set, which is relationship marketing. And that has to do with e-mails, a blog, list-building, audio, video, and web sites.

However, the process I'm teaching is how to build those relationships. Something that you could think about when you look at a niche you're considering is, What is something that you're passionate about, and what are the problems that you have with that? Let's say you're a dog trainer, let's say you have figured out a way to train German Shepherds to be great family dogs and great guard dogs.

If you've solved that problem, that's something you can build a business out of.

My suggestion is to look at things you're passionate about, look at the problems you've had and solved, and then write about it.

Those problems and solutions will be the things that you use to attract people to your list.

PAT: And if you do it that way, you'll attract the right people. They're interested in your niche.

Okay. We've gone through the steps and we're ready to start building our list.

Let's talk about relationship marketing. I want to talk about that from two angles. You need a relationship with someone else, so that they'll tell their list about the free thing you're giving away. Then you need to establish a relationship with your subscribers.

CRAIG: Absolutely. You don't need a ton of subscribers. You just need people who are focused on the solutions you're providing and you need them to know, like, and trust you.

Once you've done this, a whole bunch of worlds are going to open up for you. First of all, you can find yourself in a position of never having to work for someone else. If you have a couple of thousand subscribers, depending on your expenses, you could literally support your lifestyle by just doing that the right way.

Then you can build relationships with other people who you can recommend to your list—then, you become a joint-venture partner.

All of a sudden there are opportunities everywhere.

PAT: Let's talk about joint ventures (JVs). This is a way to make money, right?

CRAIG: Yes. Let's just say that you have a list of subscribers. They know you and expect to hear from you about Portable Empire concepts: how to make money, how to run their business so that they can be mobile and essentially follow their inspiration in life instead of being tied to a desk or a cubicle.

I may have a book or a video or a web site, and I come to you and ask you if you'd be interested in promoting this to your subscribers for some form of percentage of the profit. I think they'll be interested because your list needs to know about relationship marketing. And you would then say, "Okay, I'll check that out."

Let's say it's something free. A downloadable e-book about the essential things you need to know about relationship marketing. And you give that, for free, to your subscribers. And they say, "Wow, Pat's a cool guy. He just gave us this free content."

Part of the purpose of that book would be to tell your subscribers about me and what I do. And part of it might be to tell them about my home study course on how to build relationships starting with finding a niche through how to make money with your list.

And anybody who buys that course from me, who had gotten my e-book from you, is going to result in a commission for you. This is a very common format, it's ethical, and it's great because your subscribers get value, you look good because you gave them the free content, and I'll give you a percentage of my home study course sales, and you make money that way.

By doing this, a number of things happen.

By giving my e-book to your list, I'm going to set it up so that your list is going to have to go to my web site and enter in their name and e-mail address to download the free book. Doing so, I'm building my list. And because they went to a special page to download the e-book, I know they came from you.

I've created a valuable relationship for three different parties: myself, you, and your subscribers. Everybody's winning in this situation, and everything is voluntary—so there has to be an incentive. There's got to be something in it for you, something in it for the subscriber, and something in it for me.

That's what most people mean when they say "joint venture." I can be a one-time thing or something we agree to do over and over.

I've made all sorts of money with my friends this way. And it's always nice to make money with your friends. It adds another dimension to your relationship.

Of course, follow the golden rule. Do what you say you're going to do, pay your JV partners, don't offer crappy products—all that stuff. Make sure the process works before you ask somebody to promote your web site.

Things will go wrong. So what? Move on. Dust off.

PAT: Okay. Let's look back. You're sitting there with an autoresponder and there's nothing in it. So to build your list, create something of value that people in your niche would want, and tell other people in your niche.

It is really better if you can walk up to somebody you know. You don't want your first contact with somebody to be, "Hey, will you hit your list for me?" It has been known to work, but it's better to establish your relationship with potential joint-venture partners before you ask them to promote for you.

However you get there, by bringing something of value to somebody else's list, you can build your list. Once you've got a list of people interested in that list, you can continue building these relationships. At that point you can market to your list, feed them more information—you're building relationships up and down.

CRAIG: If you don't have anything right now, then you're probably going to look at affiliate marketing. That's kind of like a joint venture, but it's not as personal. You just promote other people's products.

You make money by recommending that your subscribers buy another company's products. You can't really do joint ventures with that, though.

I can't go to you, for example, and say, "Look, I've got this great product called Aweber, and I'd like you to promote it to your list through my affiliate link." You can get your own affiliate link.

There are also a lot of folks selling reprint rights, where you can buy the rights to someone else's content, and in some cases you can change the name, alter the content—it can be a very good way to get started. However, it's not a great way to do joint ventures, because it's something that your joint-venture partner can buy, too.

To be able to offer value, you need something unique. For example, if you can interview experts in your niche and compile that into a book or audio course, you would have something unique—even though you're not one of the experts. You're essentially a matchmaker between experts and the people who are interested in experts.

Think and Grow Rich by Napoleon Hill is probably the best known book on personal growth and prosperity consciousness. Napoleon Hill interviewed the most successful people of his time—millionaires and billionaires—and came up with what it takes to get rich. He himself wasn't rich. He created one of the best selling books of all time, and his contribution was to pull the knowledge together.

You can do the same thing. Then you do have something you can take to a joint-venture partner that's authentic. This whole thing is a learning process. You're not going to get something for nothing. You're going to have to grow as a person, learn new things, solve problems—and that's what you do every day as you live your life.

The difference is, you put that knowledge in e-books, audio products, and videos. You're going to add value to your subscriber's life. You're going to add value to your joint-venture partner's life by offering his subscribers things that they find valuable.

It's going to take effort on your part.

I know a lot of people like to sell that concept that you can get something for nothing and everything's easy—and a lot of things are simple and easy. But the most successful people I know are willing to do the work that it takes to build relationships, build their lists, create products. Even if it's just interviewing people, you need to come to the table with something of value. Then you can cash in on the fruits of your labor.

A lot of the things that I've heard people spout out about are how to make money online, and promoting get-rich-quick schemes that really don't work.

Effective hard work following proven footsteps is the way to go, and it can go much faster than you think—and I think you're a great example of that.

PAT: It gets easier, too. The learning curve in the beginning is the hardest part.

CRAIG: That's why hiring mentors, going to seminars, and listening to audio training courses is the way to go.

PAT: Then there's the moment when you have to sit down and write that first e-mail to your new list—all these strangers. That can be pretty intimidating.

CRAIG: Yes, it can, but it doesn't need to be. But I'll acknowledge that it can be because you know that person is going to read that e-mail, and people don't like rejection. Some people don't want to find out that their list doesn't like them, so they don't send e-mails to their list. That's one of the problems people have with list marketing—people don't e-mail their lists because they're afraid of bad things happening.

It's really just like anything else. Get over it. That's not your problem. Your problem is figuring out what they want. The good news is that it's not very hard to do.

Part of my e-course is a survey, in the first e-mail, asking the reader what the biggest challenge is in their business. I want to know what their biggest problem is. Then I'll know what they want me to talk about.

If I write an e-mail that addresses their biggest problem, they're probably going to read it.

You can get a lot done without being a real expert, just by focusing on what people want. I know that my subscribers are primarily interested in how to build a list, how to pick a niche, so that's what I talk about. And that's what I offer to them. And if I've done my homework, they'll buy.

PAT: It's important to be real, isn't it? A lot of my mentoring clients have this problem, where when it's time to write an e-mail to their list it's almost like they put on their "e-mail writing" hat, and start writing in this formal, stilted way that just sounds contrived. Nobody talks like that.

I think that one secret to writing good e-mails is to pretend that you're writing to a friend.

CRAIG: Yes. E-mail copywriting is a subset of copywriting. Because it's going to be read in an e-mail program—it's going to look like an e-mail. You have to be careful what you say because there are e-mail filters that will block your e-mail from being delivered. And people have a short attention span when they're reading e-mail.

But yes, you want to talk in a friendly voice, keep it conversational, and stick with the nature of the medium, which is pretty short.

PAT: You can always send them to a web page.

CRAIG: Yes. I'm not saying to write only short copy. I'm just saying that you want to keep your e-mails short. Get them to click through to your web site or your blog.

My blog is my hub of communication for my list. The e-mails are just to get them to look at the blog, because there I can put whatever I want: I can put audio, video, affiliate links—and that stuff isn't easy to do in an e-mail.

PAT: Because you never know how it's going to look. Stuff that goes to Gmail looks different than an e-mail in outlook.

So it's really that simple to write your first e-mail. Just think of one person and tell your story.

CRAIG: And if you do that . . . I know the objection in your head right now. You're saying, "I don't like writing, and what's more, I really stink at it."

Maybe you feel that way, but I'm pretty sure you can talk. You can find a way to get your message out in your own words.

What we're saying here is probably the best news you can imagine. You don't have to be an amazing writer, or even use great grammar. Some of my teachers would cringe at my writing.

PAT: Until you tell them how much money you're making, and they compare that with what they're making teaching grammar.

CRAIG: A lot of the reasons why you might be frustrated with writing in the past might come from your formal education or your job—and you'll find that it doesn't apply here. Here you can just write the way you would in a journal or diary, or writing a letter to a friend. It's better to just be yourself.

PAT: Is there anything else that people need to know to build their list and start sending e-mail?

CRAIG: Find your niche. Do your research. Find your topic and then ask yourself, "What do I know," or, "Who do I know that knows something about this topic" and, "What are the problems that people in my niche have?"

Solve those problems and sell the solutions.

Then you need to find out who is already marketing to the people who have those problems. Those people already have lists of customers, and if you have something that's complementary, you can contact them.

There are a couple of other things you can do. You can take some of the problems and write articles about them and submit the articles to article directories or ezines. Go to www.ezineannouncer.com and submit your article there. You can also go to Google and type in article directories and see what comes up.

In that way, you're going to get articles that you write out there. I know this works. It takes a little time and effort.

If you want to spend a little money, get a very clear idea of your niche, then do some research on Google adwords, and you can pay to have people come visit your opt-in page. Tell them in the most compelling way why they should opt in to your list, and then figure out a way to monetize that list and recoup your investment.

Easy to Be Hard

How to Learn Internet Marketing by (Over)Producing Records

> **Success didn't spoil me, I've always been insufferable.**
> —**Fran Leibowitz**

It's important to be real. If you have a firm grasp on who you are—as a marketer, copywriter, author, or musician—you can speak with your authentic voice.

That's the important thing.

It doesn't matter what niche you pick, there will be other people writing about and marketing in that niche.

Cool. Those people are your future joint-venture partners. In the meantime, the thing to remember is no matter how many people are telling the story, if you're telling *your* story in *your* voice, it's going to ring true and people are going to want to hear it.

If you're telling somebody else's story, and trying to sound like somebody else—well, bluntly, why bother? Who wants an imitation?

That's the trick. From deciding what niche you want to work in, to writing your sales copy, to writing your e-mail marketing material—the hardest thing to do is keep it simple. Just tell your story like you would tell a friend.

After the interview, we hung out on the manicured lawn of his very nice house talking about the time we wasted before we "got it."

Craig has only been working in Internet marketing since 2003. To go from "unknown" to "speaking at Big Seminar 7" that fast is just amazing.

I learned a lot doing the interview.

One of the things we talked about was how hard it is for beginning marketers to get started. It's hard to believe how easy it is to crank out product, once you realize that it's easy. Realizing that it's easy is the hard part.

Since Craig's the e-mail marketing guy, we talked a lot about e-mail. I was especially interested in that moment when you've built a small list, and you have to write that very first e-mail. It can be a scary, lonely moment. Those of you who have already started building your list and developing your relationship with your subscribers know what I'm talking about.

It reminded me of when I first started producing records. Actually, in my case, there should have been a new job description: "Overproducer." As in "This CD was *overproduced* by Pat O'Bryan."

It came from insecurity and fear. I can see that, now.

If one rhythm guitar part would work, I used three. If one background vocal part would be enough, I'd use six. One time I used 28!!!

My mistake? Focusing on exactly the wrong things. I was making records to impress other musicians. Musicians don't buy records. Dancers do. Lovers do. Truck drivers buy records. Musicians get them from other musicians or steal them.

The same thing is true in the Internet marketing world. I could waste a lot of time wondering what Joe Vitale or Armand Morin think about my writing. Actually, I could get scared shirtless and freeze completely and not write a word if I worried about it too much.

Wanna know a secret?

Joe and Armand aren't gonna buy my stuff. Joe's a dear friend, and I like Armand and am looking forward to getting to know him better—but they're not my audience. You are. And your readers are *your* audience. Don't worry about the Joes and Armands of the world. They get infoproducts free—by the truckload.

Personally, I like raw music. A lot of people do.

Back in the days when I was playing—and living—the blues, the real good music was in the dives. At least in Austin. Stevie Ray was at the Continental Club, Delbert McClinton was at Soap Creek Saloon. W.C. Clark was at the Austin Outhouse. The Fabulous T-Birds were at the Rome Inn.

That's where the action was. Little smoky joints with a hint of danger and romance. Sometimes more than a hint. Of both. We were young then, and stupid.

I love the microtonal slide guitar work of Muddy Waters and the over-the-top vocals of Howling Wolf. Even some of the newer things—Ray Wylie Hubbard's last few CDs are as rough and raw as anything Lightnin' Hopkins ever did.

Lucinda Williams, Eric Clapton (when he's playing blues, he plays real blues), early Peter Green.

Of course, I like Pat Metheny, too. He plays guitar like he's been practicing 24 hours a day. On another planet. For three lifetimes.

But, especially when I was in the music biz full-time, what I loved was the "real" stuff. Raw, rough, and dirty.

My live show was always that way. Unpredictable.

Why, then, did I make my CDs and the ones I produced for others, sound like pale imitations of Steely Dan? Multi-tracked, pitch-corrected, overdubbed to absolute lifelessness?

I can remember one day when I locked myself in the studio and spent 8 hours on a 30-second guitar solo. That's sick.

Here's the movie that was going through my mind: "What will Eric Johnson think when he hears this lead? What will Stevie Ray Vaughan think?"

The fact is, if either of those guys ever got a copy of the CD, it would be because I handed it to them. They weren't my customers.

And, while we're exploring the truth, they both would have appreciated an honest and raw statement from me musically a lot more than they would have respected an over-produced, overdubbed, mess like the ones I came up with. All that production and obfuscation gave me a place to hide, where I couldn't really be criticized—but I also couldn't be seen.

Sad.

It gets worse, though. I know some very talented musicians (Terri in Houston, can you hear me?) who never got around to recording anything. Nothing was good enough. They were so concerned with what other people would think or say that they never had the guts to commit themselves to recording their music. Some great music got lost that way.

The solution: Whether you're making music, or art, or sales letters, or love letters, or writing e-mails to your subscribers, just say what you've got to say and be yourself.

I've been threatening to rerecord a lot of my songs, now that I'm not really focusing on the music business anymore. I don't have anything to lose, so I don't need to hide behind the "wall of sound."

The hard, cold truth is that I would have been much more successful if I had just been "me." Warts (and flat vocals) and all.

What's this got to do with Internet marketing? Well, everything.

And then some.

If you're sitting around, waiting to write to your subscribers—or to start building your list and your relationships—what are you waiting for?

This is another point Craig and I hammered out: even if you don't have anything new to say, the fact that you're saying it in your voice is going to make it interesting. As long as you're telling your story honestly, people are going to want to hear it. The only mistake you can make is to not start now.

Don't let the quest for perfection stand in the way of building your Portable Empire.

MASTERMIND GROUPS

> Success or failure in business is caused more by the mental attitude than by mental capacities.
>
> —Walter Scott

Joe Vitale walked into our mastermind meeting, sat down, and announced, "I want to be in a movie. I don't know anybody who makes movies, and I don't know how it will happen, but I'm going to be in a movie."

Less than a year later, the movie *The Secret* was released—starring Joe Vitale, along with several other successful authors and philosophers.

At another meeting, a very single Cindy Cashman said, "Do not tell anybody, but I've decided to become the first woman to get married in outer space."

Less than a year later, she had signed contracts with a company that was gearing up for space tourism, was negotiating multimillion dollar endorsement deals, talking with reality show and movie producers, and had found the love of her life, Mitch, who agreed to the plan.

The wedding will take place in 2008. In outer space.

My more modest accomplishments, like the UnSeminar series of events and my various book and DVD deals, were also first hatched at mastermind meetings.

Throughout this book, you'll see references to my mastermind group. There's a reason for that. It's one of my secrets for success.

I was introduced to the mastermind concept by Bill Hibbler, who, along with Dr. Joe Vitale, is the author of the definitive book on masterminds, *Meet and Grow Rich*.

In the early 1990s, when Bill and I formed our first mastermind group, I was running a recording studio in Houston, Texas. Bill found my studio and dropped by to sell me advertising space in a book he was putting together, called *The Musicians Resource*.

Shortly after that, he approached me with the idea of forming a mastermind group. It was a new idea to me, but after he had explained it, I agreed to give it a shot.

That group focused on music business related issues. We shared resources, gave each other advice, and shared our goals. Some of the goals were pretty ambitious.

I wanted to escape from Houston and open a studio in a quiet little hill-country village called Wimberley. Bill wanted to manage a major rock act and travel the world. One of the other members wanted a record deal for his band. The other two members were examining their place in the music business and contemplating finding another line of work.

What was amazing to me is that we all achieved our goals. I ended up with a studio in Wimberley. Bill went on the road as Glen Hughes' manager and did indeed travel the globe. The drummer who wanted a record deal for his band ended up with a nice one, and a tour with the band KISS.

The two members who were thinking about leaving the business did, and both have become successful in their new fields.

Later, when Bill and I both ended up in Wimberley and he asked me if I wanted to join another mastermind group, of course I said yes.

We've learned that five or six members are about right for an effective mastermind group. Smaller is better than larger. It didn't take us long to attract more members.

Our Wimberley group meets once a week. We're all involved in marketing on the Internet in some capacity. The current roster includes Cindy Cashman, Jillian Coleman Wheeler, Nerissa Oden, Craig Perrine, the two authors of *Meet and Grow Rich*, Bill Hibbler and Dr. Joe Vitale, and me.

At each meeting, we allow 30 thirty minutes for social talk. Then, in the order in which we arrived, we each take 20 minutes to report on the projects that we announced the week before, to announce new projects, and to ask for guidance and advice if we need it.

We use a timer, and we're pretty strict. When your time's up, your time is up.

Knowing that the group is going to hold me accountable is a wonderful motivator. I don't want to disappoint them, so if I say I'm going to have a sales page written by the following meeting, or some other project completed, I make sure I do.

There's a "six-degrees" aspect to our mastermind group that is very useful. I can ask, "Who knows a really good book publicist?"

Cindy might reply, "I know one in Dallas, and she's real good. She handled the publicity on my latest book."

Joe might add, "I know her, too. She's handled several big promotions for me. Why don't you give her a call? Here's her number."

In one short conversation, my group has saved me hours of research. I also know that if Joe and Cindy recommend her, she's honest and good.

That's just an example. Good information is hard to come by in the real world, and access to others who can short-circuit the search is invaluable. From what books to read to who to contact for a publishing deal to what hotel to stay in on the road, I rely on my mastermind group.

There's an interesting phenomenon that happens when two or more people get together with a common purpose. A synergy develops that is hard to explain, but I've come to count on it. Some of the ideas that come up in our meetings are definitely "out of the blue." We have no idea where they come from and often can't remember who came up with them first.

Every member of our group has achieved a higher level of success over time, with the help of the group.

Meet and Grow Rich is the definitive book on how to set up and run a mastermind group. I recommend you buy it and read it. Better yet, buy six copies, and start your own group.

COMMUNICATING WITH YOUR LIST

> **No legacy is so rich as honesty.**
>
> **—William Shakespeare**

Once you've gathered some subscribers to your list, you need to communicate with them.

Malcolm Gladwell, in his book *The Tipping Point*, divides communicators into connectors, mavens, and salesmen.

- *Connectors* know a lot of people, know a lot of people who know a lot of people, and can put people together.
- *Mavens* accumulate knowledge. You probably have at least one friend who is a maven. They're the ones you go to when you are thinking about buying something, or deciding which movie to watch, or where to stay while on vacation.

  Mavens know this stuff, and really enjoy using their deep and broad knowledge to help others.
- *Salesmen* are the skilled persuaders. They can achieve rapport and build trust quickly with a prospect. They lead the buyer from confusion to decision.

To be successful at Internet marketing, you need to be a combination of the three. As a connector, you gather people to your list. As a maven, you position yourself as the expert to your list. You want them to look to you for the newest, best information in your niche. The salesman aspect becomes important to you when you want to monetize your list.

Luckily, technology has finally gotten to the point where you can automate a great deal of the process.

WHO WOULD WANT TO READ WHAT I WRITE?

That's a pretty common question. It's usually the first thing I work with my mentoring clients on. The answer is: your subscribers.

Your list will perceive you as an expert. What's an expert? Somebody who started before you did. Your job is to stay one step in front of your readers.

Certainly, there will be people who know more about your subject than you do. They're probably not on your list. You don't need to worry about them.

The ones who are on your list are the ones you need to take care of. They want to hear what you have to say in your unique voice and style. If they didn't, they wouldn't be on your list. There's an "unsubscribe" link at the bottom of every e-mail you send, if you send it using a professional autoresponder company. Some people will click on it and unsubscribe.

That's good.

Over time, your list will be made up of the people who want to hear you talk about your topic. Those are the subscribers you want.

As you communicate with them, you're going to take them to faraway places, keep them current on the latest information in your niche, give them gifts, and let them support you.

For example, I was sitting in a castle in Germany, drinking a dark, German beer and smoking a Cuban cigar. Wrought iron tables with large candles were scattered around the wall. The walls were six or seven hundred years old, and I wish I could communicate with them. I'll bet they've seen some pretty wild stuff.

It was right before showtime, and the band and I were to play in the dungeon of this castle, which had been converted into a very authentic Goth nightclub. Much more appropriate for a band who wears black leather and eyeliner than a blues band in jeans and flannel shirts. Luckily, the crowd loved the blues, and we all had a real good time.

I can't communicate with the walls, but the dungeon has wireless Internet access. I can communicate with my list. It's easy. I'm excited about what I'm seeing and doing. There are a lot of people on my list who haven't hung out in the torture chamber of an old German castle. I want to share with them.

I'm the reporter. I've got an interesting story to tell. I log onto my blog and tell my subscribers about it: the candlelight flickering on the ancient stones, the iron rings in the wall, the stairs leading to the private interrogation chambers, which now have comfortable couches and are great for an intimate conversation.

Of course, I also mention the product that I'm currently promoting. I made a lot more money from that blog post than I made playing guitar that night.

Another time, driving down Highway 90 in deep Southwest Texas, Betsy and I passed the Judge Roy Bean (the Law West of the Pecos) Park. Curious to see the home of the hanging judge, we pulled into the park. There was a sign that said, CLOSED.

There was also a sign that said WIRELESS INTERNET ACCESS. In the middle of the desert, as the sun set behind the purple mountains, I perched my laptop computer on the hood of the car and sent an e-mail to my list. Betsy took a picture, and later I put that on my blog.

Last night, I got an e-mail from Joe Vitale. He knows I'm hiding in a hotel in Austin writing a book, so it was a short e-mail directing me to check out his video blog when I took a break.

Well, of course, I'd rather watch Joe on video than work, so I surfed over to his video blog and watched his short video from Poland. He's there on a speaking gig.

It was interesting. It's warmer in Warsaw than it is in Austin. Joe was with a Polish gentleman and they discussed history, architecture, and vodka.

With a Portable Empire, you can communicate with your subscribers from just about anywhere. You don't have to travel to foreign countries to keep your list interested, but it is a good idea to let them get to know you. You control the level of intimacy you have with your list.

Craig Perrine took his wife and three sons on a vacation to Vermont last summer. They hitched their RV to Craig's truck, and camped out in RV parks. Craig posted pictures and stories on his blog, and allowed his list to join them on their vacation.

Another example, closer to home, is a video I did as a promotion for the first UnSeminar. Since the seminar was going to be in Austin, I drove through town, videotaping some of the more interesting sights. I walked down Sixth Street, videotaping along the way. Then I posted the video on my blog. It's by far the most popular video I've done, and the easiest. To me, Austin is just the nearest actual city. To my subscribers in Australia, New Zealand, Europe, Japan, and other, to me, exotic places, Austin is exotic.

HOW DO YOU COMMUNICATE?

Joe Vitale explains it this way: "A good example is when you see a movie you really like. When you talk about it, you're going to be enthusiastic and excited.

"As you're telling others about the movie, some people would say that you're just sharing, but what you're really doing is selling, and what you're really doing is copywriting.

You're using your words to tell people how great the movie is, and how they should check this movie out."

Of course, you probably didn't make any money from that communication. Let's talk about the sort of communication that can bring you money. It's called copywriting. When you communicate with someone with the intent of selling them something, you're a copywriter.

We're all copywriters. These are the same communication skills you use when you ask someone out on a date, or convince a group of friends to try that new Indian restaurant, or to get your kids to clean their rooms.

Since this is something you're going to do anyway, you might as well learn to do it well.

You Want Your Subscribers to Know, Like and Trust You

Write like you would talk to a friend. You wouldn't want to impress a friend with your massive vocabulary, or confuse them, or b.s. them. Decide what you want to say, and then say it.

If a short word will do, don't use a long one. Keep your sentences and paragraphs short.

People buy from people they know. They buy from people they like. And, most importantly, they buy from people they trust.

In Your E-Mails to Your List, and on Your Blog, Let Your Readers Get to Know You   If you take an interesting trip, talk about it. Take pictures. Shoot some video.

Take the reader with you.

Write from your own point of view, and don't be afraid to voice opinions. Yes, you're going to offend some readers. But that doesn't mean they're going to stop reading. Trying to please everyone by writing bland copy is a good way to bore your readers.

Then, they'll stop reading.

If you're reviewing a product and you think it sucks, say so. If you're writing about a seminar you're attending, and you think it's a waste of time, say so. Your individual and unique point of view is what sets you apart from the millions of other writers online.

For example, Dan Kennedy is a very successful marketer and copywriter. He's also a staunch Republican. He talks about politics in his newsletters because that's who he is. It's his point of view. Politically, I disagree with him strongly.

He also packs his newsletter with great marketing and copywriting information. When it comes to marketing, he knows his stuff.

I certainly disagree with his politics, but I pay him every month to send me his newsletter. I feel like I know Dan, although I've never met him, because he puts so much of himself into his writing.

How Do You Get Your Subscribers to Like You?   That's easy. Put them first. Your job is to serve your subscribers.

You already know what information they want, although you should occasionally ask them, so you can stay current with their needs. When they subscribed to your list, they knew your topic and niche, and agreed to receive information from you on that topic.

When you run across a new idea or concept in your niche, tell them about it. Write articles that are interesting and useful, and send them to your subscribers. You can also go to www.elance.com and hire someone to write articles for you.

Your readers understand that occasionally you're going to try to sell them a product. That's part of the relationship.

One good strategy is to offer your subscribers "prelaunch" specials. Give them a reward for being on your list.

When you're marketing to your own list, you don't have to pay affiliate commissions. Since I usually pay 51 percent to my affiliates, I can easily afford to sell new products to my list for half price. I make the same amount of money per sale, and my readers get a great deal. Everybody wins.

You'll discover a remarkable feeling of power when you first realize that you can hit your list and generate money, pretty much at will. There will be a temptation to turn every e-mail and blog post into a sales pitch. Don't do it.

Take good care of your subscribers, and they'll take care of you.

You Have to Earn the Trust of Your Readers   This can be a tough one.

When I was promoting the first UnSeminar, I made it clear that there would only be 25 seats. After 25 tickets were sold, the promotion was over.

I sent them that e-mail late at night. When I woke up the following morning, the seminar was sold out. I don't know how many tickets I could have sold, but it was a lot more than 25. Since the tickets were $5,000, I was real tempted to keep selling them. We'd get a bigger room. We'd figure it out.

Nope. I went to the sales page, turned off the "buy now" button, and put "Sold Out" in big red letters across the top.

Long-term trust is more valuable than short-term profit. The attendees at that seminar were very aware that there were only 25 people in the room. Each one of them got individual attention and training that they wouldn't have gotten if I had sold more tickets.

Over time, each customer whose trust you've earned can be worth thousands of dollars in sales.

In Internet Marketing, You're Going to Be Communicating in Several Important But Very Different Ways

E-mails   Your first line of communication with your subscribers is the regular e-mails you send them.

Visualize your reader smiling when they see your name in their in-box. What made them smile? That's what you should put in your e-mail.

E-mails are great for short messages. If you want to direct your reader to a sales page or your blog, use an e-mail.

Blogs   A blog is a specific kind of web page. Short for Weblog, it can either be a normal web page, or you can use specific blogging software. A good free one is www.blogger.com. In just a few minutes, you can have your own blog online by using one of their easy templates.

Once you've set your blog up, be sure and register it with www .technorati.com, which is a directory of millions of blogs.

Your blog can be an extension of your personality, and a great tool for letting your readers get to know you. It can also be a very effective sales tool.

This might be a good time for you to see what others have done with their blogs. In the Internet marketing world, Joe Vitale's, at www.mr fire.com/blog is a good example of how to creatively use blogging software to get readers involved in the writer's story.

He introduces his readers to his new Panoz sportscar, which is named Francine. He writes about a conversation he had with a medical entrepreneur on an airplane to Poland. He writes about the movie he's in, *The Secret*. He's got video clips of Poland and his appearance on the *Larry King* show.

He also cleverly mixes in sales pitches, but he does it in such a way that it doesn't feel like a sales pitch. It feels more like someone is telling you about a great product they've found, and is so excited that they have to share it with you.

Sort of like when you're telling a friend about a great book you think they should read.

Over at my blog, www.Patobryan.com/blog.htm, I've got a story about a set of videos I did with Craig Perrine. I recently bought a cabin near Terlingua, Texas, and there are pictures of Terlingua, and the famous chili cook-off that's held there annually.

There are articles about copywriting, pictures from seminars, pictures of the vacation that Betsy and I took in Taos, New Mexico.

Here's a list of some other blogs that you can use for inspiration:

John Carlton's Big Damn Blog: http://www.john-carlton.com/.

Michel Fortin's Blog: http://www.michelfortin.com/.

Dan Kennedy's "Millionaire Maker" blog: http://www.dankennedy .com/cblog/.

You get the idea. Pull the reader into your blog and present your thoughts and selected scenes from your life in a way that is interesting and fun. You want the reader to be so interested in your story that they're checking back every day to see if you've added new content.

Sales Pages   You'll use sales pages to promote specific products and services. Some of mine are:

> The Lost Art of Pelmanism—www.pelmanismonline.com.
>
> The Myth of Passive Income—www.mythofpassiveincome.com
>
> "I Love You," Ho'oponopono-based audio—www.milagroresearch institute.com/iloveyou.htm.
>
> Influence 101, the Unofficial Guide to the Art of Persuasion— www.influence101.com.

As you can see, they don't have to be fancy to be effective. In the next chapter, you learn how to write your own sales page. The better you get at copywriting, the more money you'll make.

THE BASICS: INTRODUCTION TO COPYWRITING

> Press on: nothing in the world can take the place of perseverance. Talent will not, nothing is more common than unsuccessful men with talent. Genius will not, unrewarded genius is almost a proverb. Education will not, the world is full of educated derelicts. Persistence and determination alone are omnipotent.
>
> —Calvin Coolidge

What's the big secret that copywriters use to write effective copy? Here it is: Everybody is in a trance. The number of people who are self-actualized and completely aware is so small that you can discount them when you're writing sales copy. The people who are going to read your sales copy are caught up in the drama of their lives.

You might want to check out the movie *What the bleep do we know?* It's the most useful explanation of this phenomenon I've ever seen.

People are living inside their heads.

They just drove home from a job they hate to a spouse who doesn't understand them, or understands them far too well. Their bratty kids are whining about some silly thing. The bills are due and they don't have the money to pay. Their mind is anywhere but where they are.

Or . . . They've spent the entire day changing diapers, mopping floors, and watching daytime TV. Their mind is on the cross-dressing librarian they couldn't tear themselves away from on the box, their feet hurt, and they're worried sick about some movie star's love life.

Or . . . The limo driver was late, the board meeting was hell, and Warren Buffett just dumped his holdings in their publicly traded corporation, and is advising the world to do the same. The SEC is skeptical about last year's financials and the little weasel in accounting who threatened to squeal hasn't been at work in three days.

Your mission, should you accept it, is to know exactly who you're writing to, and walk a few thousand miles in their shoes. Get inside their mind. Find the pain, and then frame your solution to soothe their pain.

I've seen grown men cry as they sat at their desks, visualizing their readers and their readers' lives.

That's the big secret.

Now, let's look at the nuts and bolts of copywriting. We're going to focus on the "big seven" components of a well-written sales page.

1. Headline
2. Bullet-points
3. Subheads
4. The Body
5. The Guarantee
6. The Close
7. The P.S.

Once you master those, you're ready to start writing copy.

THE HEADLINE

Ninety percent of your effort should go into writing your headline, because 90 percent of the effectiveness of your copy depends on it.

Write a lot of headlines. Fifty aren't too many.

The purpose of the headline is to pull the reader's mind out of their daily trance, and into your sales copy.

Professional copywriters, who are an educated, savvy bunch, read the magazines you find at the checkout counter at the grocery store like textbooks. "Elvis Marries 2-Headed Space Alien In Shotgun Ceremony!" "World Ending Thursday, 7:13 P.M., According To Secret Prediction!" "Oprah Loses 250 Pounds Eating Ice Cream—You Can, Too!"

That sort of thing.

Why? Because they stop you in your tracks and make you want to know more. Intellectually, you know they're bull poop, but people don't buy with their intellect, they buy with their emotions.

There are an infinite number of ways to approach the writing of headlines, but let's confine ourselves to five good ones for now.

The Question

Ask a question that can't immediately be answered with yes or no.

"Do You Make These Seven Copywriting Mistakes?"

You can't answer that unless you know what they are. You have to read the first sentence of the copy to find out. You want to know, don't you? What are those mistakes? Do you make them? What are you going to do about it?

Let's try another one.

"How Can YOU Fire Your Boss?"

Again, you won't know if you don't read the first sentence of the copy.

"What If You Could Double Your Sales In Ten Days?"

You can turn simple sentences into questions:

"You Want Financial Security, Don't You?"

"She Deserves The Best, Doesn't She?"

Here's a special kind of question headline:

"What Can A 29 Year Old Bottle-Washer From Cleveland, Texas Teach You About The 17 Shameful Secrets Of Shampoo?"

How can you resist?

The Call-Out

This is the easiest headline you can write, and it's very effective if your product is for a specific niche.

If you're selling a headache remedy, try "Headache Sufferers!"

If you're selling guitar strings, try "Guitar Players!"

If you're selling investments, try "Investors!"

You'll only get the attention of the very narrow group that you call out, but if your product is that tightly focused, that's all you need.

A Little Psychology

One of the psychological tools I discuss in *Influence101* is Social Proof. You can get your copy of this audio home-study course at http://www .influence101.com.

Humans are herd animals. If "everybody" is doing something, then "you" must need to do it, too. Everybody else can't be wrong, can they?

History is full of examples of everybody being wrong. This is the principle of Social Proof and it explains how peer group pressure works.

The fashion industry, the soft drink industry, the religion industry, and the politics industry know this one, and use it all the time, because it is so powerful.

We can use this principle to craft effective headlines.

One that has been overused lately, but is a good example is the "Who Else Wants To _____" headline:

"WHO ELSE WANTS TO MAKE $20,000 A WEEK?"

Another way to use it is:

"DON'T GET LEFT BEHIND!"

OR: "20,000 BLIND ALBINO AVIATORS CAN'T BE WRONG!"

Intellectually, you know that they can. Writing sales copy has nothing to do with the intellect. People buy with their emotions and justify it with their intellect.

Imagine That . . .

Create a Picture That Draws Your Reader In

Like:

"IMAGINE HOW MUCH FREEDOM YOU'LL HAVE WHEN YOU MASTER COPYWRITING!"

"PICTURE THIS—YOUR FIRST MILLION DOLLARS!"

The trick here is to paint a vague picture that is enticing, and let the reader fill in the details.

In the headline "Picture Yourself In The Car Of Your Dreams!" the reader will do exactly that—providing the make, model, year, and color for you.

The more detail you provide, the tighter your focus and the smaller your potential target.

Quotes

Anything with quotation marks around it will stand out.

"THE BEST CIGAR I EVER SMOKED"—Britney Spears.

"ALL MY MEN WEAR LEVIS"—Elton John.

"THEY LAUGHED WHEN I SAT DOWN AT THE PIANO, BUT WHEN I BEGAN TO PLAY . . ." This may be the most famous headline in history, by the way. It ran, successfully, for decades.

Steal This Ad

As you start thinking like a copywriter, you'll start noticing advertisements from a different perspective. Pay special attention to the headlines that get used over and over. Major advertisers are constantly testing headlines. If you notice an ad that runs for several months with the same headline, write that headline down!

It's working.

An interesting thing to note about successful copywriters: They steal. Every copywriter worth his salt has something called a "swipe file." This is where they put copies of ads that they like. When it's time for them to write a headline, the first thing they do is go to their swipe file and try to find one they can modify to fit their assignment.

Advertising may not be the oldest profession—although, it's closely related. It has, however, been around a long, long, long time. Occasionally, some genius will come up with a headline that hasn't been used before, but it's very rare. Trust me, start snagging great ads and start your own swipe file.

Caveat: Don't steal word-for-word. Use your swipe file for inspiration. As you read the ad, see if you can analyze it to discover why it worked, and use that knowledge to create one that will work the same way.

Another interesting thing about copywriters: They sue. For example, there have been instances where a copywriter has been so impressed by Ted Nicholas' copy that he used it verbatim. He regretted it almost instantly.

BULLET POINTS

There are at least three kinds of readers:

1. Those who will read every word you write.
2. Those who skim, focusing on headlines, bullet points, and major points.
3. Those who read the headline and then skip to the offer.

They all read the P.S., by the way.

As you design your copy, you need to keep all three readers in mind. You need to tell your story with your headline, subheadlines, bullet points, and P.S., for the benefit of the skimmers, and you need to do it in a way that allows your copy to flow smoothly.

Bullet points are used to call attention to benefits.

Do you know the difference between a feature and a benefit? It's a little tricky, but it's a distinction you need to learn.

- "Fine German engineering allows this car to cruise at 120 m.p.h." is a feature.
- "You can be playing golf while the others are still driving," is a benefit.

Here's another example:

- "This vacuum cleaner has suction pressure in excess of 9,000 p.s.i." is a feature.
- "This vacuum cleaner will get your carpet so clean your neighbors will turn green with envy." A benefit.
- Actually, "Your neighbors will turn green with envy" is a benefit of the benefit "will get your carpets so clean."

Are you starting to see the difference? The feature is the description. The benefit is what it does for you.

Let's look at another one.

- "This pizza contains broccoli, spinach, and spirulina," discusses features.
- "Healthy pizza for building strong, sexy bodies," discusses benefits.

Now let's look for a benefit of the benefit:

- "Healthy pizza that will make you so strong that girls will be asking you out." The benefit of the benefit "so strong" is "girls will be asking you out."

One of the most famous copywriting stories comes from David Ogilvy. He had to write a sales page for a luxury car. Writing good sales copy requires intense research. He interviewed engineers and sales staff. He examined the car.

Finally, he read the technical reports. Over a hundred pages into a dry, boring technical report he came across the sentence, "At 60 miles per hour, the loudest sound you'll hear is the ticking of the clock."

He used that as his headline. Notice he didn't say a word about the engineering excellence of the car or the seals around the windows. Those are features. He found the hidden benefit.

Bullet points are only slightly less important than headlines. Almost all of your readers will read them. If you need 10 bullet points, write 100, and then choose the best 10.

SUBHEADS

Subheadlines are like bullet points, but they stand alone and introduce a new section of copy.

Everything we've discussed about headlines and bullet points applies to subheadlines.

Use them to grab your reader by the shirt collar and make him or her read the following copy.

Here are some examples of subheadlines:

- "But Wait—There's More." Personal note: whenever I hang out with copywriters, I'm silently watching the second hand on my watch. It's only a matter of time before one of them quotes this subheadline, and then the others laugh uncontrollably.
- "New For 2007!" Would be a way to introduce benefits and features that have been changed for the new product year.
- "How can a 165 year old technology revolutionize your sales path?" is a subhead that was used for our very successful "Think and Grow Rich Automatically" sales page.

- "Living a Lifestyle Beyond the Dreams of Avarice" helped us sell a pile of The Myth of Passive Income. (www.mythofpassiveincome.com)

Get the idea? A subheadline is just like any other headline, except it leads into a specific section of copy. When you're writing your list of potential headlines, be sure and note the ones that would make good subheads.

THE BODY

This is the meat and potatoes of your sales copy.

This is where you identify your customer's pain and provide them with the magic secret that will make the pain go away.

You may be wondering, How long should the copy be? The answer is, as long as it needs to be. There is a rule of thumb that states that the more expensive the item you're trying to sell, the longer the copy needs to be.

Don't be afraid of long copy. Remember your three kinds of readers. A person who is contemplating a purchase, especially the purchase of an expensive item, wants to know all there is to know about the item.

The very first step is to visualize who you're writing to. What trance are they in as they begin to read?

What did they do all day? Was it fun? What do they want to do? Are they hungry? Are they thirsty? Are they broke? Are they looking for the perfect diamond ring?

- You've used your headline to stop them in their tracks.
- You've listed a few bullet points to make them curious.
- You've got their attention with your subhead.
- Now, you've got to lead them to the bottom of the page and help them press the "buy now" button.

Try to meet them where they are and take them with you. Imagine their objections and address them in your copy.

Avoid using big words when smaller words will do, and adjust your vocabulary to fit your reader. If you're advertising reverse amortization mortgages in the secondary market, you're going to use a completely different vocabulary than you will when you're selling diapers.

One way to pull them into your copy is to tell them a story.

I've used this one several times.

"I used to be a broke blues guitar player, living on $30 to $50 a night, a few nights a week. I lived in a mobile home, until it got repossessed. I know more ways to cook pinto beans than anybody else in North America, because pinto beans is about all we could afford to buy at the grocery store."

Hopefully, by this point in the story, I've got my reader nodding his head. He's been broke before. He's identifying with my story, and putting himself in my place.

He's ready for some good news:

"Then, one day I met Dr. Joe Vitale at a restaurant in Wimberley, Texas, and he handed me that book. What book? *Spiritual Marketing*.

The secrets contained in that book gave me the knowledge and power to reframe my life, and create a lifestyle that gives me freedom, happiness, and pleasure."

If I've done my job, my reader is asking, "Where can I get that book?"

Your story doesn't have to be about you. It does have to draw the reader into your sales copy. Use your story as an opportunity to stress the benefits of the product in a personal way.

Another strategy for writing compelling sales copy is to round up your best sub-headlines and put them in a logical order. Then use your copy to expand and explain the benefits mentioned in the subhead.

Let's look at some other strategies for leading our customer to the "buy now" button.

Problem–Solution

One technique I rely on a lot is the "problem–solution" copy.

You might start out by asking a question:

"Do You Suffer from the Heartbreak of Dandruff?" for example.

Then describe the heartbreak of dandruff. Maybe tell a story about a man who lost his wife, his job, and his self-respect because of dandruff.

That's the problem.

Then, just before our poor dandruff sufferer hangs himself from a shower rod, you present the solution.

"Rub this duck oil on your head twice a day, and you won't have to worry about losing your wife, your job, or your self-respect."

I'm exaggerating just a little. The gym where I work out has a TV, and today I went during the day, when the soap operas were on. Daytime TV is pretty educational, if you're a student of advertising.

I'm not exaggerating very much. For certain audiences, that approach works like a charm.

With appropriate modification, it will work for any audience.

Testimonials

The sales copy can contain testimonials, or you can use them to break up the copy into sections.

Testimonials are essential. Instead of just one person (you), who has a financial interest in the sale, telling them how great the product is, you can gather a crowd to tell them.

The two best kinds of testimonials are from experts and people just like your customer.

There is a trick to getting a testimonial, even from an expert, by the way. It's a secret, but I'll tell you.

You ask.

Don't tell anybody.

Use testimonials to build the case for your product.

THE GUARANTEE

Use your guarantee to shift the risk from the purchaser to you.

You want your customer to feel totally confident when they buy your product. If they feel like they're going to be stuck with it if they don't like it, they won't buy it. This is especially true on the Internet, where they can't touch or even see the actual product.

Here's a rule of thumb I learned from a very famous copywriter who was speaking at a seminar: "The longer the guarantee, the lower the return rate."

Think about it. If you know you've got three days to decide if you like something, you're going to be in a pretty big hurry to find something you don't like. If you know you've got a year, or a lifetime, you don't feel any urgency. In fact, you may forget about it completely.

I believe in strong guarantees.

I watched Joe Vitale offer a "double your money back" guarantee on a product that sold for almost a thousand dollars. That's a very gutsy guarantee. It worked. He sold almost half a million dollars worth of product in just a few days, and one of the reasons was that outrageous guarantee.

Clickbank, and most merchant account companies, keep a reserve to pay for refunds. They use an algorithm based on your refund history, the price of the product, and the phase of the moon—I guess. I really don't know how they do it, but I do know that they keep part of the sales revenue for a long time to make sure there's money there to pay for refunds.

It's worth it.

THE CLOSE

This is where you ask for the sale.

There's no point being shy now. Either you've built a strong emotional case for your product or you haven't. You're about to find out.

Ask them to click the "buy now" button.

The trend right now in online sales is to hit them high, and then offer a lower price.

Like this:

What would you pay for that kind of freedom? What's your financial independence worth to you?

You're probably thinking, "At least a million dollars."

And you're right—but because you're one of my treasured subscribers, I'm offering it for only $497—But Wait, There's More!

If you buy today, or anytime before next Tuesday, you can have our guide to financial freedom for only $17—But hurry, this is a limited time offer.

Again, I exaggerate for effect—but all the pieces are there. Establish a high value for your product and then give a believable reason why it's cheaper in your offer. Create a sense of urgency, and stick to it. If you say that the price is going up on Tuesday, make darn sure you raise the price on Tuesday.

The close is where you mention the bonuses.

Whenever another author asks me if I've got anything lying around they can use for a bonus, I always answer yes, even if I have to write it specifically for their project. Most marketers and authors are the same way.

Why?

Because we embed links to our web pages and our products in those bonuses. They are an excellent tool for driving traffic to our web sites. The more traffic, the more sales for us. You will have no trouble gathering up as many bonuses as you need.

Let's say you round up 10 e-books as bonuses, and can realistically valuate them at $30 each. That's $300 in bonuses that you can give away that didn't cost you a cent.

Those bonuses will make your "close" a whole lot easier to write. Like this:

Buy "Grow Tomatoes Automatically" for only $17, and get these bonuses, valued at $300, absolutely free!

Remember, people buy with their emotions and justify the purchase with their intellect. What sort of emotional response do you think you're going to get, when you offer to trade $317 worth of product for $17 in currency?

Bonuses make sales.

THE P.S.

After you've asked for the sale, you sign the sales copy and go home, right? Wrong. One of the most important lines on your sales page is your P.S. Put it right under your signature.

Everybody reads the P.S.

This is where you restate the most important aspect of your sales letter. Like this:

P.S. There is no risk on your part—our products are guaranteed for your lifetime, and the lifetime of anybody who looks like you. Buy now!

Or: P.S. Don't wait—offer ends tomorrow!

Use the P.S. to convince the reader who has passed right by the "buy now" button to retrace his steps and buy.

Some copywriters will add a P.P.S. and a P.P.P.S. I don't know if there is an upper limit to the number of these things that can be used effectively. I try to limit myself to two.

INTERVIEW WITH DR. JOE VITALE

To help us fully understand the science and art of copywriting, I interviewed Dr. Joe Vitale. Joe is a best-selling author, movie star, and TV personality. He's also one of the most respected and expensive, copywriters on the planet. His rates for writing a sales page start at over $25,000 and go up fast.

Joe was kind enough to spend an afternoon talking to me about copywriting. We sat in his kitchen, at his estate in Wimberley, Texas, while we recorded the following interview. Since his hourly rate is $2,500, the rest of this chapter is easily worth over five grand. If you use the information wisely, it can be worth much more than that.

Enjoy.

PAT: Let's talk about copywriting. Let's assume that the reader knows nothing at all about copywriting—just totally clean and new on the subject. We need to give them enough information so that they can go from zero (I don't know what copywriting is) to writing a believable, effective, first draft of a sales letter.

JOE: I think the first thing is to define what copywriting is, just in case somebody doesn't know. Copywriting is writing the words that create the sales message. In other words, in an ad, the words on the page are called copy. On a sales page, the words are called copy, and when you write those words you are considered a copywriter.

And of course, the same thing is true on a web site. All the words and all the text on that web site is copy. So, copywriting is the text to persuade somebody to buy from you.

PAT: Like a little salesman you can replicate who goes out and tells your story.

JOE: Once you put it out there, it pretty much stays up and keeps on working, and will work night and day while you move around the world—which is part of the secret to creating your own Portable Empire.

PAT: What is the first thing I want to do? I have a product, I want to use a sales letter to sell it. Is there any mental work I need to do?

JOE: Oh boy, that's a great question. And I say "oh boy" and roll my eyes because there's a tremendous amount of mental work that has to be done. Research is one of the most overlooked areas when it comes to copywriting. The average person just picks up a pen (or turns on the computer) and starts writing the letter, thinking that's what they have to do to be a copywriter—but it doesn't start there at all. It starts before you ever pick up the pen. You have to pick up the product and become intimate with it. You have to pick up the book, or audio product, or whatever it is you're trying to sell. You should know it inside and out. If there's research to be done, you should be doing every aspect of research that you can think of, because you want to know more about the product than you can possibly imagine you'll ever use.

You need to become the expert on it, and that may be the case already if you created the product.

The other part of the research is "who is the product for?" Who are the people who will be reading your sales letter? What is on their mind? Are they men or women or young or old? Are they of a particular nationality?

You have to know as much as possible. What keeps them up at night? What are their problems? What are their concerns? What are the stones in their shoes that are hurting their feet?

You want to know their problem as well as you can. If it's possible, I would say you would even want to talk to that audience. This goes into market research. You may or may not want to go this far. But when somebody hires me to write a sales letter it's not uncommon for me to find out who's in that target audience and try to find a sampling of that target audience to find out truly what they are thinking.

If I can find out what they're thinking about this product, that will help me be a better copywriter when I finally pick up the pen or get in front of the computer.

As you can see, all of this happens before you ever write a word. This is all the research step, which is the very first thing that has to be done.

And I would imagine the very next thing is to be aware of what is the benefit of having your product or service. I think most people are far too concerned with what they are trying to sell, and not thinking about what people are being asked to buy—and there is a difference. The fundamental, zenlike shift that I ask people to make is to get out of your ego and get into your prospect's ego.

This is really tough, because we are really married to our egos. Most of us don't realize what our ego is, and what part of it is our ego and what part of it might not be our ego.

We want to completely separate ourselves from that and get into the other person's shoes, and start to imagine what will they get from this product or service. How will it enrich their lives? How will it benefit them? How will it help them sleep better? Or lose weight or get healthy or make more money? Whatever the benefits happen to be.

And you can even go a little deeper than that and find out what the benefits are of those benefits. So if you have a product that is, say, "This product will help you make more money" then, what's the benefit of having more money—to that prospect. There's a deeper benefit than the obvious.

This is getting into advanced copywriting, so I'm just going to leave it as a seed here.

What you want to be thinking is, who is the audience, what is the product, how does the product help them, and the mental shift you want to be thinking about is getting out of your ego and into their ego.

This is all before you pick up the pen or turn on the computer.

So this is the legwork. The brain work. The research work that has to be done that is the foundation to becoming a great copywriter or writing a piece of copy that is truly persuasive.

So from there, I would be thinking about the headline.

So in my mind and the minds of the great copywriters I've studied like John Caples to Bruce Barton to David Ogilvy to Gene Schwartz—any of the ones you could name—they all say that the headline is the make it or break it point.

And if you think about it, as people are darting through the newspaper looking at headlines or they're darting through a magazine or they're zipping along on the Internet—all they see are the headlines and maybe some graphics.

If the headline doesn't convey something that stops them, they're going to keep going. They will never read your copy.

As brilliant as it may end up being, if the headline did not telegraph to them some benefit, some curiosity, some humor, some sort of message that clips their mental process and stops them in their tracks, so that they read your copy, then your copy is going to be pointless. You might as well have nothing there.

So, headline is of primary importance, here.

A good headline is going to come from that research that you've done beforehand, when you were thinking about what your product is, how it serves the people who are going to get it, who the people are, and what their problems are.

When you start thinking about those, you'll start to narrow in on what the benefit is.

Now, I have some tricks when I write headlines.

One of my favorite ways to write a headline is a "how to." Just simply "how to."

We mentioned money earlier. It could be "How to Make Money," "How to Save Money," "How to Do Anything." Fill in the blank. If you think about your product or what it does for your audience, if you put the words "how to" in front of whatever that benefit is, you've begun the headline.

You may not settle there, but in terms of what we're trying to accomplish, this will get you started. You can tweak it, but you can write a good headline just by beginning with "how to."

How to do something, how to solve something, how to achieve something, how to . . . fill in the blank.

PAT: What are some other options?

JOE: Another headline that I like is the question headline. This is one of my hypnotically favorite ones. I use it myself a lot.

The question you ask in the headline has to be done in a particular way. I like to ask a question in the headline because it engages the mind of the reader. But if you ask a question in your headline that can be answered with a yes or no, the chances are that they will answer with a yes or no and not keep reading your copy.

So what I do is very hypnotic. I ask people a question that they cannot answer without reading the sales letter. And again, this is right off the top of my head—might be something like "Which of These Seven Secrets Will Help You Save the Most Money on Your Taxes?"

Now, I just made that up, but you can imagine that an accountant came up with it; maybe it's selling a tax-relief book.

PAT: Like "Do You Make These Mistakes in English?"

JOE: Another famous one is "Which of These Seven Mistakes Do You Make in English?" which is a very different headline.

I'm glad you brought that up because "Do You Make These Mistakes in English" can be answered yes or no. You can just say, "Yeah, I make mistakes in English. So what?" and move on.

But if you say, "Which of these mistakes do you make in English?" I cannot answer the question unless I read the copy to see what it refers to.

The word "which" draws me in, and hypnotically it opens up my mind so that I'm much more curious. Curiosity is very powerful, from a hypnotic standpoint or from a persuasive mind-opening standpoint.

So that's another trick that you might use, just to ask a question in the headline. And again, that question needs to be one that's open-ended, that they can't answer unless they read the copy.

Another way to write a headline is to use a testimonial as the actual headline.

If you've got a product or service that's already out there, and people have been telling you, "I really love your cupcakes," or whatever they've bought from you; when people tell me compliments about my books or my software or any of my programs I say, "Thank you, can I have that in writing?"

Usually, they're glad to give me an endorsement because they just told me how much they like it, and that sincerity is there.

Sometimes, if they're a little reluctant to write it, I'll offer to write it for them, and give it to them to sign off on, which is a way to make it easy for them.

Well, if it's a one- or two-line endorsement, that's very strong, very specific, and very clear—that can be your headline.

One of my favorite, easy ways to write an entire sales letter—this is another inside trick that I use myself—is if somebody writes me a testimonial that's a few paragraphs long, I will use that as my sales letter.

I will say, "Instead of me raving about my product, or new book, look at what these other people are saying." That leads right into the testimonial.

Then, I'll add a close to the end of it, tell them where and how they can get the product or book, and sign off—and I've effectively written a sales letter.

And this is an innocent but effective way to write a sales letter, if you've already got, or can get, some endorsements.

But, going back to our way of writing a headline, all you need is a one- or two-line endorsement from somebody. It does not have to be from somebody people know, it just has to be from a real person.

It needs to be specific, detailed, concrete, and that real person needs to give their full name. Don't just use initials. If possible, use their photo with it, use their web site with it, and if they'll let you, put their phone number and e-mail with it.

All of this is to build credibility. But that simple one- or two-line endorsement can work as your headline.

PAT: And you're actually letting somebody else write your sales letter for you.

JOE: I'm all for that. I'm looking for any way to cut corners.

Even if you're not a professional copywriter, you can use these insider tips to go around the corners and find the shortcuts—and write it without writing it, in a way. That's what this is all about.

PAT: Some people write 30 to 50 headlines, and then choose the best, and then harvest out of that list for their subheadlines and headings. Do you do that?

JOE: Yes I do. I work very hard on my headlines. Even on my blogs. I have a blog up now that I'm very pleased with. When I'm writing my blog, I treat it as a piece of sales copy.

When I looked at blogs when I first heard about them, I was very skeptical. I couldn't figure out why people were looking at these things. They're very self-indulgent, ego-driven, like diary entries. The headlines don't have much of a headline.

I thought, "I'm going to apply copywriting techniques to my blog."

I know that people have a tremendous amount of choices. I need to captivate their interest before they'll read my material.

So in order to captivate their interest on a blog, just like on your sales page, or in your flyer, or ad, or anything you do to promote your service or product, I need the headline to sing.

I need the headline to stop people, grab them, and pull them in. So that's what I'm doing, even on my blog.

This should tell you something—if I'm doing this on my blog, where I'm not trying to sell anything directly, then how much more important is it for you to do it with your sales letter?

When I go to write a headline for anything, I may generate 12-30-50, I've done as many as 100 different headlines. Looking for the one that I think really sings, that will stop people.

And often, by generating that many headlines I'll find that there will be two or three that I can combine together.

You can surprise yourself by finding out things about your product that you didn't know you knew.

PAT: You're coming up with a treasure chest of ideas that you can use throughout your sales copy.

JOE: Yes. And we're just talking about communication here. But honing your communication so that people pay attention to us and get what we're trying to say. That's what this is all about—and it's fun.

PAT: So we've thought about it, we've got a clear visual image of who our customer is and why he should buy what we're selling. We've got our treasure chest of ideas, from which we can pick out the best one, and put it at the top of the page.

What next?

JOE: Well, Joe Sugarman is a famous copywriter and marketing legend.

The guy behind the famous blue-blocker sunglasses, and I'm pleased to say that he's a friend and mentor of mine.

He says that the only purpose of the headline is to get somebody to read the first line of your sales letter. And he says that the only purpose of the first line of your sales letter is get somebody to read the second line of your sales letter. And the only purpose of the second line . . . all the way down to the end . . . where you get them to buy from you. Where you ask for the order.

And that's the essence of what this is all about.

So, the headline stops them. The beginning of the first line needs to pick up where the headline began, and walk people through— generating interest, telling them the benefits, explaining to them why they're going to enjoy having this product or service.

You're going to be relying on all the research so you are clear why they would really want this. You don't want to imagine why they would want this; you want to be able to nail it. You know they have a particular problem, and your problem or service is going to solve that particular problem. And you want to say that in your copy.

PAT: You've got to come from integrity—you can't sell something you don't believe in.

JOE: Absolutely.

PAT: That's an important distinction to make. I'm not sure that all copywriters make that point. Especially when they're selling and teaching copywriting.

JOE: There are some ruthless copywriters for hire out there who will sell anything. But in my book, the *Seven Lost Secrets of Success*, one of the lost secrets is sincerity.

Sincerity sells.

People have a built-in b.s. detector. You can fool some of them some of the time, but you're not going to build any rapport and you're not going to have a long-term relationship with them, so you're not going to get the long-term sales.

If you want to build a Portable Empire, not only should you be making sales, and customers, you should be making friends, who are sending you money for the rest of their lives and your life.

You've got a beautiful win-win relationship, and that's only going to come if there's built-in trust. The fundamental truth in psychology is that people buy only from people they like. People they know, like, and respect.

So if you are lying to them and they catch on to it, you've broken the rapport and you've broken the relationship. Never, ever, ever come from insincerity.

I say that sincerity is a lost secret. Sadly, when you look around, there are a lot of people in business, too many people writing ads, too many copywriters who are willing to sell something that needs improvement before it's being offered.

PAT: So the first step is to believe in your product before you do any of the rest of this stuff, and if it's not right for your customer, pass.

JOE: Absolutely. You have to take it to the right audience.

You know, when you talk about sincerity, this goes back to one of my inside secrets, and that's enthusiasm. If you really believe in your own product or service, you should be excited about it, you should be in love with it, and if you're in love with it, you can't wait to tell the people who would most benefit from having it.

A good example is when you see a movie you really like. When you talk about it, you're going to be enthusiastic and excited.

As you're telling others about the movie, some people would say that you're just sharing, but what you're really doing is selling, and what you're really doing is copywriting.

You're using your words to tell people how great the movie is, and they probably want to check this movie out.

That's what you need to infuse into your copy. You should be as passionate, in love, and enthused about your product or service as you are about a movie that you really like. When you have that kind of enthusiasm, that kind of energy, and that kind of passion—and it stems from your heart, it stems from your sincerity—then, writing your sales letter is far, far easier.

People also read sales letters and pick up on energy. This is the attractor factor kicking in here.

But on a vibrational level, on an unconscious level, you are communicating things you are not even aware of. And people are listening and reading and picking up on things that, on some level, they're not even aware of.

If that connection isn't there. If you're not totally in agreement, congruent with the product that you're trying to sell, the other person will not pick up on it.

So writing good copy comes from sincerity, it comes from passion, and at those points the headline becomes easier to write, what you want to say becomes easier to write, asking people for the order becomes easier—because all of this flows from a very natural state.

So I'm actually giving you more clues about how to write the sales letter.

I want you to almost throw away all formulas and come from one formula: When you speak from your heart with sincerity and passion, you will touch the other person's heart, and that will awaken their interest in buying your product or service.

If the product matches their need, the sale should be a snap because, at that point they'll be drooling, saying, "Just tell me where to order, just tell me where it is."

PAT: I want to make a comment here—something I picked up from my coaching clients. A lot of them seemed to put on their "I'm going to write a sales letter" hat, and suddenly adopted this stilted language.

From watching you, and learning from you, I think you would agree that it's important to write like you're talking to a friend.

Keep your vocabulary, your word choices, your sentence structure, the same way you talk.

JOE: You would write it exactly like you were writing to a friend. That's one of the inside tips for something like this.

Here's what I do: I imagine I'm going to write about the product or service to a friend of mine who is on the mailing list. I will just pick somebody in my mind and visualize them.

I write as if I were talking on the phone or in person, just one on one.

One of the big mistakes that people make is they put on the hat that you were just talking about, and they start writing in a wooden kind of language—like it needs to be a certain way. Like they were trying to please an English teacher from a long time ago.

They think they're writing to the entire world. They think they're writing their copy to the entire world, and that becomes very intimidating. The secret here is that when you write your copy, you write it to only one person, and when they read it—even if a million people read it—they read it one person at a time.

They read it feeling like it was just written to them.

So you write your sales letter as if you're writing it to one person. When thousands read it, each one of them will feel like you wrote it to just that person. That's often how I write my e-mails, where tens of thousands of persons receive them. You won't believe how many people write me asking if I wrote it just to them.

They won't know, because I wrote it so personally.

It's not that I'm trying to deceive anybody, it's that the writing has an intimacy level that comes from me writing as if I'm writing to just one person. It's just being shared with lots of people.

That's how good writing is done. I say throw away the dictionary, throw away that hat that says COPYWRITER on it, throw away the English teacher who might still be haunting you, and freely express yourself.

Find what you're excited about in your product or service and express that.

PAT: Let's talk about the framework we're going to put this philosophy on. I know there are no rules to copywriting, but if I were writing my very first sales letter, I'd want a framework. I'd want to know that the headline goes at the top, the first sentence leads to the first paragraph, we're going to have some bullet points . . . we're going to use testimonials if we can get them.

JOE: You're covering most of it right there.

PAT: I'm just setting it up for you.

And, of course, we're leading up to what is probably the number one most asked question about copywriting: How long does it have to be?

Let's build our infrastructure—the framework we're going to put this philosophy on, and let's build from that.

JOE: There are several things to talk about here. Here's my advice. Take everything that we've talked about: speaking from your heart, throwing away the copywriter hat, getting rid of your inner English teacher and speaking from enthusiasm, speaking to your target audience.

Sit down and write the first draft nonstop, without thinking. Meaning: turn on your computer, put your fingers on the keyboard, and just start writing. Just write nonstop. Don't think about it. Don't edit yourself. Don't stop to look up facts, figures, words, anything— just let it go.

Get your first draft done. You may get it done in 20 minutes. It may take an hour. The promise you make with yourself, which is guaranteed to work, is that once you start writing, do not stop for anything until you have finished the first draft.

If necessary, if you don't know what to write next, write: "I don't know what to write next." And you know that your mind will give you something to write—write it down. Just keep going.

The deal is to write the first draft nonstop. There are reasons for this: You'll blast through any blocks if you do this. Studies have also shown that your creativity will increase; your use of metaphor will increase. All the things you worry about—spelling, punctuation, grammar—they'll get better.

You won't even have to worry about them, because you're trusting your unconscious—the right side of your brain—to handle this for you.

Whether it comes out good or bad or garbage—that doesn't matter. The point is to write your first draft.

After you've written your first draft, reward yourself. Have a cup of coffee. Dance. Play guitar. Whatever you do for fun. Walk around. Jog. Lift weights. Whatever you want to do.

Then, come back, because now you're going to edit. You invite your ruthless high school teacher or whoever taught you punctuation. You can put on your editorial hat. Go through and correct the grammar. Find where you wrote, "I don't know what to write next," and take that out. Wherever you were unsure about the spelling, or the date, or punctuation, plug it in.

Fix all of that so it's reading more accurately, and you're comfortable with it.

Okay, now take another break.

Now, come back and restructure it so that it looks like a sales letter. You have a whole lot of words here, and you're probably comfortable with most of them.

Put your headline at the top of the page. That's traditionally where it goes, because when the eyes first land on the page, they're going to see what's at the top and what's biggest. The headline should be big and bold and at the top.

Underneath it, you may have a subheadline. Remember, we generated dozens or 100 headlines. Some of them may be usable. You may not like them as much as the headline that you use at the top of the page. Those could become bullet points or subheadlines. You might have a subheadline under the main headline.

Then, you're going to go into the body of the letter. Begin it with "Dear Friend." That has been tried and it's true that it always works. If you can personalize it, do so.

In the case of not being able to automate that, or know who's going to be reading, you just say "Dear Friend." It will be unconsciously accepted by people because they see it so much.

Now, of course, you have the body of the letter, but you're going to break it up. Short sentences, short paragraphs are the rule of thumb in copywriting. I like to make the first sentence just a few words, if possible.

If I make it a sentence, I keep it short—say 50 characters or less.

These are rules of thumb that you're welcome to break later, but this will get you started. Use short paragraphs.

I like to use dialog whenever possible, because those quotation marks signal to the brain life, energy, and something happening. We've learned that from all the books we've read in school.

Not enough copywriters know this technique, but it's very hypnotic and you should use it.

How do we use it? Maybe a testimonial, you could tell a story about somebody who's used your product or service, and you might tell the story with somebody talking. You spoke to somebody and they said something back.

Put those in quotes, telling a good story.

Move through all of this, breaking up the text, because, remember, you might have written several pages, and you want to break it up so that it's visually attractive. If it looks overwhelming when people glance at it, few people will work that hard.

You want to make it easy for them. Break up the text. Use one- or two-line sentences. Use short words.

After you've written five or six paragraphs, short paragraphs, consider breaking that body up with another headline. That's called a subheadline.

You're making the page look very attractive and very easy to read and very smooth to look at.

It's visually enticing.

Do this all the way through your sales letter, and of course, you're building interest, telling what the benefits are. You may have a list of bullet points—answer the question, "What do I get," or "What happens when you buy this product or service?"

Tell them what the benefits are, always, always, always getting out of your ego and into their ego.

Toward the end of the letter you should have a "call for action." This is when you're finally going to say, "I know that you want this. Here's how to get it."

It could be an order button, a phone number, an e-mail address, a snail-mail address—be sure to have a call for action.

Somebody has to sign this letter. It needs to be your name or whoever the letter is from.

Remember, the people reading this need to feel like you wrote it to them, so it's a real person who signs it, not a company.

I always add a P.S.

If you look at my blog, which is not a traditional sales letter, you'll find a P.S. on every post.

PAT: Sometimes more than one.

JOE: Sometimes five or six. And one day I didn't know what to say, so I wrote, "Have you ever noticed that you always read these P.S.s?"

People do read the P.S. They read the headline. Some of them skim the letter, which is why you have bullet points and sub-headlines, because they're gathering on a sensory level some of the material that you're trying to communicate to them, and they'll always jump down and read the P.S. So the P.S. is another opportunity for you to hit them with another benefit, another reason to buy; maybe it's a limited offer before the price goes up—you're encouraging them to take action now.

Maybe there's another call to action.

There's nothing wrong, in my opinion, with having three P.S.s, but if you start to go over three, and I've done it, it weakens the power of them.

This is just Joe's rule of thumb—you can break my thumbs later and do it your own way. For now, I'd say three P.S.s are fine. Be sure that each one counts. You have to be ruthless when you're editing all of this, because you know these people have other things they can be reading. I know it.

They might be fans of my work and have read other stuff by me, but if I bore them, if I don't promise a benefit, or if I write a sales letter that has some boring lines in it, they're not going to stay with me. They're not going to stay.

I have a rule of thumb that's in the back of my head all the time. I think it's a quote from the novelist Elmore Leonard, that says, "I try to cut out the parts that people skip."

So when I'm reviewing my own writing, sales letter, blog—whatever it is—I'm saying to myself, "Will they skip over this? Is it important?"

Of course, I'm doing a little psychic work here, because I'm trying to mind read. But that's how I do it, and I think a lot of good copywriters do it that way. We're trying to second-guess where the people are going to get bored or disinterested; we either have to rewrite it so that it's much more interesting, or we have to kill it.

That's the overall method and structure.

Now, how long should it be?

PAT: Yes. When do you know you're through? If I'm excited about something, I can write 50 pages, but I may be able to tell my story in a paragraph.

JOE: Well, this argument has been going on for over 100 years. If you get the graphics people and the copywriters in the same room, it really gets heated. The graphics people want more space for the pictures and the word people want more space for the text—and they fight it out.

The rule of thumb is to say what you have to say and shut up. If you can truly do it in a paragraph, do it in a paragraph, and turn off the flow. It doesn't have to be any longer.

The way that I explain this to people is that if I said to somebody listening, "_____, I would like you to have lunch with me today," that's all I would have to do.

Unless _____ doesn't like me for some reason—she probably hasn't met me—she'll probably say yes.

So I don't need much copy. I sold them on lunch.

If I say, "_____, I would like you to meet me for lunch, and I want you to buy," I might need to add a line, maybe not. Depending on how they perceive our relationship.

If I say, "_____, I want you to meet me for lunch, I want you to buy, and I want you to bring a check $5,000, made out to me," she's going to need an explanation.

And that's where I have to put in longer copy.

So in my mind, the higher the price for something that you're asking the person to buy, the longer the copy needs to be.

If you're trying to sell chewing gum, and it doesn't cost very much, and you can explain why this chewing gum is different from other chewing gum, you can probably do it in a paragraph.

But if you have a time-travel machine, and it's guaranteed to work, but it costs $250,000, you're going to have to do a lot of explaining. That's when long copy has to come in. It depends on the circumstance.

JOE: Here's a last trick. After you've written your sales letter, make 12 copies of it. Share it with 12 people. It's important that they're not your family members or immediate friends, because they are not your target audience.

If you have a mastermind group, or access to a target audience, send those 12 copies to them, and invite their editorial feedback.

There's one more trick to this. When the feedback comes in, look for the majority vote. If just one person makes a comment, you can take it or leave it. If they all get confused by the headline, or don't understand what you're trying to sell—that's priceless feedback.

Go write the letter again, before you release it.

Product Creation

Product creation is where the magic happens. The wizard flicks his wand, and—out of thin air—a product appears.

Where can you find product ideas? The trick is to remember that every problem is a product. There are problems everywhere. Once you start thinking like a product developer, you'll see them and welcome them.

What used to be an irritation is now an income source.

Once you've chosen your niche, it's a breeze to find problems. You're looking for problems that cause a lot of pain for a large group of people. That pain is going to make you rich.

Forums are good for this. A web search on "your niche" and "forum," will locate them for you. Hang out (lurk) and see what problems are being posted to the forum.

One of the best ways to maintain your expert status and to come up with new product ideas is to continue learning and growing in your niche.

If your niche is, for example, building wooden furniture, keep learning new ways to build wooden furniture. Experiment with exotic woods. Recreate designs from the past. Learn the most recent innovations.

Note the problems as you run into them. You'll solve them naturally as you learn.

That's where the magic happens.

When you've got a Portable Empire, you're an information merchant. Your thoughts, solutions, and ideas are your stock in trade.

There are at least four kinds of products that you can sell to your list.

1. Products you make yourself.
2. Products anybody can sell (www.clickbank.com is a good place to find these).
3. Products you acquire through joint-venture agreements.
4. Products you purchase resale rights to.

Let's take a closer look.

PRODUCTS YOU MAKE YOURSELF

This is my favorite, because if I sell my product to my list, I get to keep all the money. I can also approach other list owners and create a joint-venture arrangement where they sell my products to their list. We split the money, and I grow my list. We talk about product creation in depth in just a moment.

PRODUCTS ANYBODY CAN SELL

Clickbank (www.clickbank.com) is the largest and best known site for these products, but there are others. I like Clickbank. They have a huge directory of products that anybody can sell. They handle the payment from the customer, credit the seller and product developer with their percentage of each sale, and send checks twice a month. Clickbank makes going to the mailbox fun.

Once you've built your list, it's a good idea to keep an eye on the Clickbank directory. You can find products that fit your niche and offer them to your list. It's not as effective as offering products you create, but the quality of products can be very good, and it's fast and easy.

Remember that you're doing your list a service when you do this. As long as you're coming from integrity by confirming that the product is beneficial to your subscribers, you're earning your commission. Hint: Most product creators will give you a copy of their product, if you explain that you're considering promoting it to your list.

Don't ever promote a product you haven't personally seen and used. Ever.

I use Clickbank both ways. I register a lot of my products there so that other marketers can sell them, and I occasionally market Clickbank products to my list.

You can have a lot of fun with Clickbank. I'll give you an example. A couple of years ago, Betsy and I decided to take a weekend vacation. We rented a suite in a nice hotel on the River Walk in San Antonio, Texas. We ate some amazing Mexican food and enjoyed margaritas in a cantina right on the river.

As an experiment, I decided to see if I could get my list to pay for the vacation. I was still new to Internet marketing, and I knew it would make an interesting story for my blog, even if the promotion didn't raise enough money to pay for the vacation.

When we checked into the hotel on Friday, I went to Clickbank and found a few products that fit my niche. Over the weekend, I promoted them to my list.

The experiment was a raging success. By sending a few e-mails, I more than paid for the trip.

This is a cool technique, and some people base their entire business on this model.

PRODUCTS YOU ACQUIRE THROUGH
JOINT-VENTURE AGREEMENTS

What is a joint-venture agreement? In this case, it's a simple agreement between a list owner and a product owner.

The list owner agrees to promote the product to his list for a percentage of the sales. When the list owner offers your free bait to his list, that's a form of joint-venture.

Once you've built your list, you're in a position to "JV" with other product developers.

Just like the Clickbank example, it's important to check out the product before you promote it to your list. If it's an e-book, read it. If it's an audio product, listen to it.

When you're on the list side of a joint-venture, your primary goal is to safeguard your relationship with your list. Your secondary goal is probably to make money.

It's important to keep these goals in the correct order. By carefully screening the products you offer to your list, you're building trust and a positive relationship.

Over time, by putting the trust aspect first, you'll make a lot more money than if you focus on money. Your list will grow, your conversion rates will increase, and your profit will skyrocket. People buy from people they know, like, and trust.

If you promote products that aren't a good fit for your list, or worse, are defective, you lose that magic know, like, and trust relationship.

PRODUCTS YOU PURCHASE RESALE RIGHTS TO

Some product developers will allow you to buy their products, rebrand them, and sell them as your own. This is a quick and easy way to acquire products to sell to your list. Of course, the original developer will try to sell as many copies as they can, which means that you'll run into a lot of other people selling the same products.

The same rules that apply to JV products apply to resale rights products.

You can find some great products this way, but you have to be careful. Get a copy of the product and make sure it actually works. Some marketers use resale rights sales as a dumping ground for their products that have bombed. You don't want to market those products to your list.

If it's an e-book, read it. If it's an audio product, listen to it. If it's software, use it—before you offer it to your list.

WHICH FORM?

Your product is a solution to your customer's problem. How will you present your solution?

This is a question you'll run into when you're developing products.

The easiest answer is to honestly determine how you communicate most effectively. Are you a writer? More of a talker? Do you have video skills?

I use a combination of all three but, because I like to write, I end up using e-books and articles to get my information to my list, most of the time.

The quickest and easiest way to get your information to your readers is to use your autoresponder. You can create an e-course by writing a series of articles, or dividing your book into sections, and delivering them sequentially over a period of time. You could tell your autoresponder to send a chapter or article every other day, or once a week.

E-books are an easy way to get your information out there. Anybody who can access the internet can download an e-book. In terms of file size, they're tiny. They download quickly.

What Is an E-Book?

Technically, an e-book is a PDF file that your customer can download from the Internet. Here's how you make one.

After you've done your research, write down the solution in the form of an article or short book. Thirty pages is a good length for a short e-book. You can make it as long as you like, but your reader will valuate it based on how well it solves their problem, not by weight.

Once you've got it written, convert it to a PDF file. You do this using a PDF generator, which acts like a printer. However, instead of printing to paper, it prints to a file that you can upload to the Internet and others can download.

There's a free one at www.pdf995.com. Open office, at www.openoffice .com, also has a good word processing program and a built-in PDF generator.

Most computers come with a PDF reader. You can get a free one at www.adobe.com.

Audio is just a little bit trickier. The simplest solution is to acquire an MP3 recorder. You can record yourself reading or talking, or interviewing someone, and load the file to your computer. From there, you can transfer it to the Internet, where your customers can download it.

Since I come from a music background and just happen to have a recording studio, I use the same audio software I use to create my music products.

You can get a free audio editing program at www.audacity.source forge.net, which is almost as good as the program I use, which cost hundreds of dollars.

The end result is the same. However you create the audio file, you need to convert it to an MP3. They are the Internet standard for audio downloads, and almost all computers come with software to play them.

The LAME MP3 encoder is a free solution for converting audio files into MP3s. Do a web search, and you'll find several sites where you can download it.

Video can be even trickier than audio. Right now, about half the world is using dial-up to get online. Downloading video on a dial-up connection is impractical; it just takes too long. So, right now, if you strictly use video, you're going to miss out on half of your potential audience.

That's going to change, and change fast. Interestingly, the rate of change is also increasing. Very soon, I predict that broadband Internet access will be universal, wireless, and much faster than what we're using now.

For now, I recommend that you use video to augment your e-books and audios. Videos have a higher perceived value than audios and e-books, and, judging by the success of online video sites like YouTube, they're going to be what we use computers for in the very near future.

There are several ways to deliver video. The most common are Flash, Quicktime, and Windows Media. They're probably already on your computer. If not, the players are available as free downloads.

For our purposes, any consumer video camera will do. Some of them come with editing software. If not, there are some good ones from Adobe, Pinnacle, and Sony that cost less than $100. They will all allow you to edit your video and save it as either a Quicktime or Windows Media file.

If you find you enjoy delivering your solutions in a video format, you may want to invest in better cameras and editing software. A good 3-chip video camera, a Mac tower, and Final Cut Pro is what we use.

It's important to remember that your bait is information. For the purposes of attracting subscribers to your list and selling them solutions, it really doesn't matter how you deliver the information.

Find the medium you're most comfortable with. The important thing is to get the bait online.

PRODUCT CREATION DATA FORM

The secret of successful product creation is to create products that people will actually buy. To do this, you need to find out what problems the potential customers in your niche have, and then offer the solution.

Go to www.Google.com and do a search on "forum" and your topic. For example, if your topic is golf, do a search on Golf forum.

List the ten most active forums here.

1. _____

2. _____

3. _____

4. _____

5. _____

6. _____

7. _____

8. _____

9. _____

10. _____

EVERY PROBLEM IS A PRODUCT RESEARCH FORM

Surfing through your forums, note what problems the other members are talking about. What are the most common problems? What problem is causing them the most pain? Which problems can you solve easily and quickly?

Find the problems that you can turn into products and list the top 10 here.

1. _____

2. _____

3. _____

4. _____

5. _____

6. _____

7. _____

8. _____

9. _____

10. _____

For the other "how to" chapters, I interviewed an expert on that topic. For product creation, I'm the expert that other people interview, so I interviewed myself.

HOW TO
CREATE PRODUCTS

———

A lot of people get bogged down about product creation. I've had conversations with people who have been working on their e-books for years and had just about settled on the title.

Others spend months and months doing research, without ever writing a thing.

I want you to understand: You can create a viable, marketable product in an hour. And then you can make another one.

You might think that there's really no need for another product online, and wonder what you can bring to the market that's not already there. I used to think that way.

The fact is, the online marketplace will support unlimited numbers of products on any subject. What makes your contribution unique, and valuable, is that you'll be telling your story and providing your solution to a problem—in your own voice.

For example, hundreds of people have written e-books on how to write e-books. I've written one, myself. They all sell, and most of them are actually valuable resources. The reader might find one insight in Jim Edwards' book, another in a book by Armand Morin, and a different point of view in my book. They're all good.

The difference is the voice and point of view of the author. Some people respond to my writing style, others to Jim's—and some people will respond to your style.

The trick is to realize that this is easy, and just write your e-book or create your product in the same way that you'd tell a friend about it.

It's important, when you're writing, to send your internal editor away. We've all got an internal editor. It could be the voice of a grade school teacher, with her red pen for marking spelling mistakes. It could be a family member telling you that what you've got to say can't be important.

There is a time and place for the editor to do their job, but it's after you're through writing. Whenever you hear that critical voice while you're writing, acknowledge it, and let it know that you'll appreciate its input at the proper time.

Then send it away. Ignore it. Just create.

Once you train yourself to look for them, product ideas are everywhere.

Product creation is simple. You find a problem and solve it. Then you sell the solution.

That's it. It really is that easy.

If it's hard, you're doing it wrong.

Find what works, and do that. Identify what doesn't work, and don't do it.

So that you can quickly and easily get your first product online, I'm going to recommend that you start with writing an e-book.

Writing e-books is easy, fast, and you can do it over and over again.

I'll also talk about other ways to make products—but let's start with e-books.

Remember, the whole trick of creating a Portable Empire is to create multiple streams of passive income. That's why I love e-books. They don't cost anything to make, you don't need a warehouse to keep them in, and they don't cost anything to deliver.

I'm going to show you how to write an e-book. Fast. There is no limit to the number of e-books you can write, and once you catch on to how easy it is, you can knock out one a day, if you want to. E-books are easy to write, and easy to sell.

So, let's go over the basics, and then start knocking out product. Your product needs to be part of your overall marketing strategy. Everything you do to build your Portable Empire needs to work together to maximize your results.

Your first step is to decide what niche you want to work in. It's okay to have several niches, eventually, but when you're first starting out you need to coordinate your list, your free information you use to build your list, and your product.

You're going to be tempted to try to market Internet marketing-related products. Resist this temptation. Don't do it.

Later, after you've made your third or fourth million from Internet marketing—that's the time to teach people how to get rich on the Internet.

Until you know how to do something, don't try to teach it. Your credibility will be shot—possibly forever.

There are ways around this, though. Remember, we're marketing to a parade. There are always people entering the Internet marketing world. Those are the people behind you in the parade.

An expert is somebody who started before you did. To the people who start after you, you're an expert.

You can market to them, and still maintain your credibility, as long as you're teaching them something that you actually know.

For example, when I discovered how easy it was to write e-books, I immediately put together an e-book to teach others how to write them.

For now, you're probably better off choosing a niche that you already know something about. Later, as you run into problems in your own life and solve them, you'll have new subjects to write about.

To give you an idea of what kinds of e-books are selling, let's go to clickbank.com. That's www.clickbank.com.

Click on "buy products." Now click on the subject titles and explore. See if you can find a pattern.

The e-books that appear on that first page are the ones that are selling the most. Some top-selling e-books are bringing their authors six figures a month in income. Let's look at some of the titles on the first page of a few categories.

Right away, you'll notice that "how to" is a popular subject.

- How to buy cars at auctions.
- How to play slot machines.
- How to swing a golf club.
- How to buy real estate at auctions.
- How to train a dog.
- How to speak French.
- Recipes—this is a big one.
- How to play guitar.

- How to get a job.
- How to get spyware off your computer.
- How to lose weight.
- How to cure bad breath.
- How to jump higher.
- Cure heart burn.
- Cure acne.
- Hypnotize.
- Clean your computer's registry.
- Copy DVDs.
- Get gorgeous.
- Grow hair.
- Stop snoring.
- Kiss.
- Stop panic attacks.
- Beat stress.

These books are all selling enough to make it to the front page on Clickbank—that means they're moneymakers.

Okay. The first thing you need to do is pick a topic. There are two schools of thought on this subject.

The first, which is the way I usually do it, is to pick a subject that it would be fun to write about. If you're fascinated by race cars, write about race cars. If you're in love with Barbie dolls, write about that. There are over six billion people on the planet, and over a billion of them are online. Odds are that any subject you pick will be interesting to a group of people.

The value of doing it this way is that you'll enjoy your work, write more e-books, and write them faster. It's a way of fooling your subconscious into thinking you're playing when you're working. It works for me.

The other school of thought is to do research to establish where the greatest demand is, and write an e-book on a topic you know people are interested in.

They both work.

If you're going to go the research route, the easiest way is to find out which books are at the top of the Clickbank list and write a book on the same topic.

Another great tool for research is Alexa.com—www.alexa.com. Go there and click on the right side of the page where it says "movers and shakers." That will show you what web sites are most popular, and will give you plenty of topic ideas.

http://www.Google.com/press/zeitgeist.html is a great resource. It shows what the most popular searches are on Google—what people are the most interested in.

Another trick I use, when I'm at a loss for a topic, is to hang out on forums. Go to a place on the Internet where people gather to talk about a subject, and see what questions they ask.

Do a Google search on your topic and the word "forum." For example, if you're interested in tennis, go to Google.com and type in tennis forum. When I just did that, I got over 40 million web pages. It's unlikely that they're all relevant, but that still gives you a lot of options.

Go hang out at the forum. Scan the conversations. See what questions you find.

I just did that, and landed on a forum where tennis pros and teachers help younger players. The first question I saw was from a beginning high-school player who asked: "How do I choose a tennis racquet?"

Then several pros answered the question. And they disagree. And they don't give any information on what they based their recommendations on.

The guy who asked the question is probably more confused than he was before.

There's an e-book there.

Remember: this may be your first e-book. Maybe not. Either way, write it fast. That's the important thing. Don't go for perfection. For now, don't worry about grammar or punctuation. Just write it.

The important thing to remember is that it is definitely not your last e-book, or your last product. You reputation does not hang on this one narrow thread. This is just an exercise in product creation.

Once you've finished your first one, and have discovered how easy it is, you'll be able to do it over and over again—and that's the goal, to build your Portable Empire with multiple income streams.

Once you've chosen your topic, how are you going to write your e-book?

One strategy for producing an e-book quickly is to ask others to write it for you. Some of the most successful e-book promotions have featured e-books with multiple authors.

Get online and find the authorities on your subject. Contact them, and ask them to contribute a chapter to your book.

Why would an author give you a chapter for your book? Because you will encourage them to include their contact information and links to their web pages, that's why. The more copies of your book you sell or give away, the more traffic they get to their sales sites. More traffic equals more sales. This technique works really well when your potential authors have a strong web presence—and actually can make money from the increased online traffic.

I used this technique when Joe Vitale and I wrote *The Myth of Passive Income.*

We sent out e-mails to people who were authorities on making passive income, and who made their money at least partially online, and asked them to tell us about their normal passive income day.

It sold really well, and it's still selling.

That's probably the easiest way to write an e-book—have other people write it for you.

Another really easy way to crank out an e-book is to have a conversation with someone who is an expert.

- Record that conversation.
- Transcribe it.
- That's an e-book.
- Put it on Clickbank and sell it.

This is a really cool way to make a product fast—and there's a hidden benefit. You've actually made two products.

You can take your recording and convert it to MP3s, and sell those on Clickbank, too or make a combination of the two and sell them together.

There are a lot of good candidates for this. Some topics I think would benefit from this type of treatment are:

- Dating
- Auto mechanics
- Nutrition
- Health
- Investments

- Kissing
- Skateboarding
- Playing video games
- Gambling

But I'm just going down a list of experts that I know to come up with those topics. Who do you know that's an expert?

Remember, there is no board of certification involved in this. An expert is somebody who knows more than the people who are going to buy your e-book.

The last method we're going to look at is using lists to write your e-book. This is a fun one. Here are some lists I came up with for an e-book:

- 25 tricks for saving money on gasoline.
- 101 e-book ideas.
- 10 steps to the perfect cup of coffee.
- 17 things you must know about wine.
- 99 great sandwich ideas.
- 19 things to look for when you're looking for a computer.
- 111 dating tips for the shy man.
- 1,001 ways to make money with your laptop computer.
- 12 secrets of automobile maintenance.
- 25 things your banker will NOT tell you.

Each one of those titles solves a problem.

To write the e-book, make a list. Let's say we're writing the book "25 things your banker will NOT tell you."

Start out with your list of 25 things you want to tell the reader. These could have to do with borrowing money, investing money, avoiding fees—people have a lot of fear about bankers, and money in general.

Now, put the first item on your list at the top of a blank page. In this case, let's use "some banks provide free checking accounts" as our first tip.

Now write a few paragraphs on how some banks charge for checking accounts, some banks don't charge if you keep a minimum balance, and some banks don't charge at all. Maybe give a few examples.

Congratulations. That's chapter one.

Now, take the second tip and do the same thing.

Okay. Now you've got three methods for writing an e-book:

- You can ask others to submit chapters.
- You can interview an expert.
- Or you can make a list.

Of course, you can also do something completely different or combine these strategies.

Some authors have rituals that help them write. At some point, it comes down to you and your computer. No matter which method you choose, you're going to have to organize the data, write some connecting text, create a table of contents, and format your book.

Sometimes, you'll write an article like this one, where you're just tapping into your own mind and putting your thoughts on your hard drive.

I tend to like to work in informal settings. I'm writing this in my living room, sitting on the couch. Mozart on the stereo. It's comfortable. I've got some good French roast coffee and a nice cigar.

Sometimes I need stimulation, so I write in a coffee shop. I can write a while, and then watch the people. There's an especially interesting coffee shop in Austin where I go to write. There is a covered porch, and a carnival of interesting people walk in and out of my line of sight.

Other writers have different styles. One of my friends has an office/fortress where he locks himself away to write. He's got his reference books on bookshelves, a very fancy chair, two monitors for his computers.

Other writers book a hotel room to get away from distractions.

I've done that. I pick a place I'd like to visit and book a hotel room. Then I write my book—and explore a new town, find new restaurants, and treat it as a working vacation.

You'll find what works for you. You may need a fortress and a library, or you may just throw your laptop computer in a backpack like I do and head for someplace interesting. There are no rules, and there's no wrong way to do it.

The important thing is to write. Get the e-book done, get it online, and then sell it. You can make enough money from a well-marketed e-book to pay for lots of hotel rooms—and houses and cars and vacations.

But first you have to actually write the e-book.

How long should an e-book be? Long enough to solve the problem. I've seen e-books as short as 20 pages. The longest one I've written is 120 pages.

Your customer isn't going to be counting words. Your customer has a problem, and they want a solution.

There are lots of ways to make your e-book appear longer. E-books don't kill trees, and there's no manufacturing cost—so there's no reason to try to save paper.

You can use your e-book to promote your other products and web sites. In some of mine, I just copy the sales pages from the Internet into the e-book.

A cool thing about e-books is that you can have hyperlinks. If the reader is interested in learning more about one of your other products, all they have to do is click on the link, and they're automatically taken to the sales page, and the ever-important "buy now" button.

Most Internet authors use Microsoft Word when they write. When I first started out, I used a less expensive program that I liked a lot—but I immediately ran into problems when I started co-writing. My co-writers were all using Word, and we had some nightmares trying to convert my files so that they could add their contributions.

I finally just bought Microsoft Office. It truly simplified my life as an author.

Another option is a share-ware program called "Open Office." You can get a free copy at www.openoffice.org. You can use Open Office to create word documents that Microsoft Word users can open and add to.

Once you've got your e-book written, how do you turn it into a PDF file, so that it can be downloaded—and sold?

The best program I've found, and the one I use, is made by Adobe. You can get a copy at http://www.createpdf.adobe.com. It's not free.

There is a good free program that converts word files to PDF called PDF995. You can download it at www.pdf995.com.

PDF995 is clumsy, compared to Adobe—but I used it for about a year, and a lot of my e-books were created with it. It works fine—Adobe works better.

At our seminars, we hand out copies of Open Office. You can download it free at www.openoffice.org. It has a word processor that is similar to Microsoft Word, and a very good PDF generator.

Once you've got your e-book in PDF form, you can put it online and sell it. We'll talk about how to do that later.

Now, let's look at some other ways to create products.

I've already mentioned audios. If you know how to get audio onto your computer's hard drive as MP3s, you know all you need to know to make audio products. You can sell audio downloads on Clickbank, too.

I've got a music background, and I've owned a recording studio for years. When I first started recording music, back in the dark ages when we still used tape and the final product was on vinyl, it cost over $100 dollars an hour to record music.

Today, you can get good audio recording equipment for under a hundred dollars, and record all the audio products you want.

MP3 recorders are good, because you don't have to do any file conversions. You can just download the audio from your recorder to your computer, and from your computer to the Internet.

With the popularity of Ipods and other MP3 players, audio products are hot right now, and that's a trend that's going to continue. If you want to spend a little more, you can increase the quality of your product dramatically.

I just did a search on free audio editing software, and I'm a little surprised to find out that there are some really good ones that you can download immediately—and for free at http://audacity.sourceforge.net/.

You can use editing software to take out the "you knows" and the "uhs. I use a program called Sonar, which is the same program I use to make my music CDs. It cost several hundred dollars, and is way too complicated if all you want to do is edit spoken word audios.

Sony Sound Forge is another editing software that is simple and popular. I just found it online for $25. If I didn't already have Sonar, I'd use Sound Forge. If there is such a thing as an industry standard for online audio, it's Sound Forge.

Another thing to look at when you're making audio products is the quality of your microphone. Today, when you can buy a good large diaphragm condenser mic for $50, there's no excuse to use a bad microphone. And you can really hear the difference.

A small investment in a microphone preamp and a dynamics compressor will make a large difference in the quality of your audios. If you find out you like making audio products, you'll want to explore these things, but they're not necessary. The customer is buying the content. As long as your audio is audible and not distorted, you'll be fine.

That's the technical side of the equation. Now, what about the creative side?

WHAT KIND OF CONTENT WORKS AS AN AUDIO PRODUCT?

Interviews and conversations work. Also, a product like this one that focuses on teaching a specific skill. Really, any topic that you could write an e-book on you can also read into a recorder. You can double your products and your income, by offering an audio version of every e-book you sell.

If you're going to keep your empire portable, you should stick to digital downloads. Convert your audios to MP3s, and let people download them just like they would download an e-book.

You can also burn your audios to CD. If you're going to deliver physical products like CDs and DVDs, I recommend that you use a fulfillment house to do that for you.

A good fulfillment house will duplicate your products, package them, and ship them for you, for a fee.

As online access speeds continue to increase, it's getting much easier to deliver video and audio online. You can automate the entire process, so that once your system is in place, you don't have to deal with anything more complicated than depositing checks in your bank account. That's true passive income.

If you want a Portable Empire, concentrate on creating passive income streams.

Videos can also be delivered online, just like e-books and MP3s.

I've done a few video training videos, and I've found they're not hard to do. With a decent digital video camera and some free software, you can get video online.

The thing to remember when creating a video is that you're selling information. Even if your video quality isn't quite Academy Award material, the focus is on the quality of the information.

I initially used a small consumer-grade video camera to capture the video, and inexpensive software to edit it. The total investment was less than $500. Over time, I invested in a couple of very good video cameras, and a professional editing suite.

I used to say that video was the wave of the future. Now, it's the wave of the present. We had our first six-figure month when we released the videos of UnSeminar1. That changed everything.

Videos can be created quickly, delivered online, or through your fulfillment house, and have a higher perceived value than audios or e-books.

There are some subjects that are just easier to explain with video, and video is great for building rapport with your subscribers and customers.

The final point I want to leave you with is that we're in the business of selling ideas. Ideas and solutions.

It's easy to get trapped in the details of product creation—and it is a trap. The important thing is to have that creative idea that solves a specific problem, and then make the solution appear.

It's the idea that makes the money.

I know a best-selling author who never writes a word. She has great ideas, and she hires a ghostwriter to write her books to her specifications. This is legal and ethical. You agree with the writer on price and terms, and after the book is written, you put your name on it as author. You can find inexpensive ghostwriters at www.elance.com, for example.

Some Internet marketers create software. They've identified a problem and visualized a software solution for that problem.

They then go to someplace like www.rentacoder.com and hire a programmer to create the software. Once the software is delivered, the person with the idea pays the programmer and puts his name on the software. There have been large fortunes made with this business model.

There are lots of other ways to create products. It's an infinite universe, and there are no rules or limits. Maybe you'll be the one who discovers the next new way to turn ideas into money.

The important thing is to do it. No matter what topic you choose, find the method that allows you to make problem-solving products quickly and easily, and then start building your Portable Empire.

THE BASICS: "O'BRYAN'S THEOREM OF INTERNET WEALTH"

Y ou've probably already figured out the basics, right? *You come up with a model that generates more than it costs and duplicate it.* That's the whole secret.

You create your first source of passive income. That's the hardest part. Once you've done that, even if it's only generating $10 a month—throw yourself a party! Because all you have to do to become financially independent is duplicate that model over and over—until you have hundreds of passive income generators spinning for you.

Here's a piece of insider information for you. If you can identify a segment of the Internet world that is experiencing pain, and relieve that pain, you will get rich.

The greater the pain + the simpler the solution
× effective marketing = $Profit

Let's call that "O'Bryan's Theorem of Internet Wealth." Somebody call the Nobel guys.

The points of pain, the solutions, and the marketing resources are available to you.

- You can buy the research.
- You can join membership sites and subscribe to newsletters.

- You can hire mentors, or join "inner circle" groups.
- You can go to seminars and develop relationships.

How do you know which one to join? How do you know which leader to follow? Which seminar to go to?

That's the easiest part. Check out the success of the people who are already in that program. That's the proof.

For example, I took on 25 people for the "Portable Empire Unseminar1." Out of that group, two went on to become major Internet marketing gurus. Several others have created successful businesses online.

I knew they were serious about becoming successful, because they committed to the cost of the seminar, the airfare, and the hotel. They committed to spending three days working on their Portable Empire.

I created the best environment I could for them to learn and gathered the best teachers I could find. I suspect that they all will become more successful.

That's the proof part.

There are a lot (a lot, a lot, a lot . . .) of people who are selling information on how to become successful online. Some of them are fantastic. Some of them are cynical jerks who are ripping off their customers. How do you know which is which?

Talk to the customers. Get the proof.

Just as an aside—it's amazing how much free information there is online. John Carlton, Gary Halbert, Joe Vitale, Dan Kennedy, Craig Perrine, Bill Hibbler, Willie Crawford, Jim Edwards, and myself have free e-books, courses, and articles that you can get immediately. You could learn all you need to know by just mining that gold.

I'm a member of Dan Kennedy's Gold inner circle. It doesn't cost much and gives me access to all of Dan's past articles and resources. It's a bargain.

(Caveat: There are some really bad programs out there, and some of them are expensive. Before you put your money down, demand to talk to people who have completed the program. Everybody's excited about their success, when they first join a program. The proof is their actual success at the end of the program.)

I remember a time, a couple of years ago, when Bill Hibbler told me he

was going to pay $2,000 to go to a seminar. I told him—well, I don't re-
member exactly, but what I thought was that only an idiot with a trust
fund would spend that kind of money going to a seminar.

Bad call.

Since then, I've attended a lot of seminars.

Good call.

It's true that the information from the stage is usually good. It really is.
It's cutting edge, best practice Internet marketing information. For example, one little trick I picked up from one of the speakers at the last seminar
probably made our business over $20,000 in about six months.

What's wild is that the information is the least interesting thing about
it. During that seminar I met the owner of a respected book publishing
company. The following week, I sent off the signed contract for my first
book deal with him.

I met David Garfinkel and Mike Stewart, hung out with Michel Fortin,
chatted with Armand, the list goes on and on. Ultimately, you'll get your
best information through relationships with people who are experts in
their fields. You can meet them at seminars.

BURN RATE

> **When you got nothing, you got nothing to lose.**
>
> —Bob Dylan

> **If you're not spending more on your shoes now than you used to spend on cars, you're not living prosperity.**
>
> —Randy Gage

> **The difference between winning and losing is timing.**
>
> —Pat O'Bryan

I guess I was lucky, in a way.

When I first started building my Portable Empire, I was debt free. My trailer had been repossessed and nobody was going to give me a credit card. My truck was paid for.

My "burn rate," or the amount of money I needed to just break even, was almost zero.

So, when I started making money, I could feel it. If I made a dollar, I could spend that dollar on new acquisitions. I didn't have to go backward and service debt with it.

I've been in debt. It sucks. It sucks your income, and it sucks your energy and enthusiasm. It's just no fun.

I'm not qualified to act as a financial advisor, but since I'm here to help you build your Portable Empire, I'm going to just go ahead and advise.

If you're in debt, get out.

As your income starts to go up, you'll be tempted to increase your spending. Wait. You can have all the toys you want, but there's a step in between. Don't skip this step.

On the subject of "burn rate," it's a good idea to revisit Robert Kiyosaki's book, *Rich Dad, Poor Dad* (Time Warner Paperbacks, new ed., 2002).

The missing step he recommends is using your income to buy investments, and using the income from investments to buy toys.

The most important investments are in yourself and your business. Books, audio programs, videos on "how to," and the mindset of success. Those are investments in yourself.

The second most important investments are in your business. You want to own the factory. You want to own the printing press. They're not expensive. Any good capital investment will pay for itself many times over.

Find a good CPA. Almost anything you buy for your business should be a tax deduction.

Initially, you need a laptop computer and some software. Most of the software you can grab for free.

As time goes on, you may want bigger computers, audio recording equipment, video recording equipment, laser printer, smart phone, or BlackBerry.

Each investment should solve an immediate problem and continue to solve it.

Why do I have six computers in my office? Each one performs a specific function. I can have video rendering on the Mac while I'm composing music on the AMD tower. One of my employees can be scanning public domain books on the little Dell while we use the big Dell to print out a rough draft of another book I'm working on.

Six computers in a one-person office may be overkill. Maybe I just like computers. The point is that you want to automate everything you can. If you can buy a computer for a few hundred bucks, and use it to increase your productivity, that's probably a better investment than $5,000 shoes. For now.

RATE OF RETURN

The difference between a smart capital investment and a passive investment is that you can multiply your rate of return with ideas.

With a $500 laptop computer, I've made hundreds of thousands of dollars. Can you think of one legal passive investment that has that kind of return?

It felt a little uncomfortable to buy a used video camera for $2,500 right before the first Unseminar. That was an expensive seminar to put on, and when I bought it, $2,500 kinda stung.

When I sold 116 copies of the videos of that seminar at $997 each, I felt a lot better about that investment. Went right out and bought another one. And a Mac tower, and Final Cut Pro, and several other video items.

Robert Kiyosaki says, "Choose your battles. And your battlefield."

There's another level to this. There really is a psychological advantage to wealth. Wealth can look a lot of different ways. What's important is how it looks to you. What makes you feel good?

Nice clothes, luxury car, gracious home, good food and drink—these are all things that can make you feel prosperous, and are appropriate rewards for a job well done.

I encourage you to explore them. But, I also encourage you to wait until you can buy them from passive income. That beautiful house will bring you no pleasure if you're fighting foreclosure. That luxury car won't be much fun if you can't afford gas for it.

Poverty sucks.

Timing is everything.

JOINT VENTURES

Let's look a little closer at joint ventures. At a mastermind meeting, Joe, Bill, Craig, and I got into a long discussion about joint venture proposals. This is a subject that my coaching clients are struggling with, and really, most beginning marketers struggle with.

It really hit home to me how lucky I was to be sitting at that table. Joe Vitale is one of the pioneers of Internet marketing, and just keeps growing from amazing success to amazing success. His goal is to be the world's first trillionaire. I wouldn't bet against him.

Craig Perrine is one of the up-and-coming gurus. The gurus all know him, and respect him. He's one promotion away from being a guru himself. He's also got a dangerously skewed sense of humor.

Bill Hibbler is one of my oldest friends. He's the one that got me into Internet marketing, and introduced me to Joe. He's quietly built up a very impressive Internet empire. He also used to manage rock stars, so we share the music biz connection.

To get these guys together for a consultation would cost thousands of dollars an hour. Let me share the wealth with you, by letting you listen in to a conversation we had about joint ventures.

There is a temptation for new Internet marketers to use the "shotgun" approach when they try to set up joint venture deals. In the shotgun approach, you send a form letter to everybody you can think of, asking them to promote your product.

We were unanimous on this. The shotgun approach never works. There. That's all you need to know about the shotgun approach. Don't waste your time.

Bill reminded me of a time, 8 to 10 years ago, when I tried the shotgun approach in the music business. I put together a promo kit, with pictures, press clippings, and my latest CD and mailed it to record companies. Wasted several hundred dollars. I got no response.

Later, I got a record deal, publishing deal, and a couple of great agents, but I didn't get them by using the shotgun approach.

Well, what does work? We all agreed that building a relationship was important.

So I asked Joe, Bill, and Craig to imagine they were sitting in Cleveland, Texas, or some other backwater spot, and they wanted to establish a relationship with a potential JV partner. What would they do?

I want to make it very clear that the first step is to identify who you want to establish the relationship with. You need to focus on each potential JV partner one at a time.

Here are the steps they would take:

1. Find them, and get on their list.
2. Subscribe to all of their newsletters and read them. You want to know what their niche is, what their interests are, and—this is very important—what they like. More on this in a minute.
3. Send them an occasional e-mail telling them that you like their ezine, and telling them exactly what you liked. Quote the ezine or newsletter.
4. Once they've responded to an e-mail, and acknowledge you, offer them a free article or e-book to use as a bonus for their promotion. It's important that your bonus has some relation to their promotion.
5. Politely ask if they'd be interested in promoting your product. Do *not* send attachments. Do *not* send a long e-mail with your biography. Do send a polite request stressing what's in it for them.
6. Repeat step five politely but persistently until you get the result you want.

I've seen this work with Joe, and I believe that it will work with most gurus *if*—and this is a big *if*—the product you want to promote is actually a great product and it is the sort of thing his customers will actually buy.

For example, Craig's customers are savvy, experienced Internet marketers who are interested in the nuts and bolts techniques of list building. My e-book, *The Absolute Beginner's Guide to Internet Wealth*, would be totally inappropriate for his list.

Joe, on the other hand, has a list of people who will find that book very useful.

Now, look at step two, where it talks about finding out what they like. Now, close the door. Make sure you're alone. I'm about to tell you a secret.

You can get a guru's attention by bribing them. This is a secret. Don't tell anybody. You didn't hear it from me.

It's true. It's the psychological principle of reciprocity in action. Here are some of the bribes that have worked:

- Single malt scotch.
- Italian leather coat(s).
- Case of oreos.
- Vintage books.
- Steak dinner.
- Gourmet coffee.
- Official baseball team cap (worked wonders with a Japanese record exec).
- Twenty-dollar bill.
- Maduro churchill cigars (I live in hope).

Note: Clever works better than expensive. You can't buy these people. You can amuse them. If their passion is coffee, and you send them a pound of blue Kona grown on a small coffee plantation, dried and roasted by loving hands—they'll think of you as they drink the coffee, and they will read your proposal. The point is that you cared enough to learn about them, and learn what they like, and send it to them. Don't go buy a hundred pounds of coffee and send it to a hundred gurus. Find the one who is passionate about coffee and concentrate on him.

Or find the one who has a sweet tooth for Oreos, and send him a case.

(*Disclaimer:* This is word of mouth. Hearsay. I have no evidence of anyone ever receiving or responding to a bribe. If I did, it was years ago and the statute of limitations has run out on it. If it ever happened. In the case of the case of Oreos, the evidence is long gone—his son ate 'em.)

A bribe will not guarantee that the guru will promote your product. However, some of these marketers get dozens of offers a day. It's a full-time job just reading the e-mails.

If you send your proposal FedEx, with a memorable bribe (remember, you've researched them to find out what they like), you greatly increase the chances of your proposal actually getting read.

It's still up to you to create a great product, and offer it to marketers who actually have access to the people who will buy it. Be sure to stress the benefits to the list owner and his list. This is not the place to give your life history or beg for help. Desperation does not sell.

A quick and easy way to build a relationship and create a product, is to interview or co-write with your potential JV partner. The less work they actually have to do, the more likely they are to agree to your proposal.

Why would you do this?

- When people see your name associated with a guru's name, there is a perception that you are worth listening to.
- It gets the guru emotionally involved in the project, and he'll do what it takes to make it successful.
- The first one is the hardest. Once you've successfully worked with one guru, it's much easier to connect with, and work with, others.
- You get to "cream" the guru's list. You can build your own list by capturing the names of people who show interest in the product you create with the guru.

This led to a discussion of other problems beginning Internet marketers have. Craig said it best, "If you are currently broke, you have no business creating or marketing success products."

The funniest JV proposal any of us has ever received said, "I've got a great marketing course, I just don't know how to market it." It's actually become famous in guru circles as the ultimate bad example.

Bill followed up. "The Internet marketing niche is full. Not only is there no room for anyone else to market products in that niche, if you do compete in that niche you're competing against the best marketers on the planet. You don't stand a chance."

I can tell this to my coaching clients until I'm blue in the face, and they'll still try it. I don't understand.

Your chance of success is higher in just about any other niche.

The trick is to discover what you're actually good at, and sell that. What are your skills? Be honest about where you are now. Craig, again: "Do you like being lied to? If you're marketing success products, and you're not successful—you're lying."

Craig had the solution. "There are two kinds of people in Internet marketing: marketers and product developers. You're probably a product developer. Find what you're good at, and make a product out of that."

This led to a discussion about product development.

It's easy. If you like to write, and you write well, it's even easier.

If you don't like to write, or don't write well, get an audio recorder and record interviews. You can record interviews over the phone. You can make videos and sell those. A cheap video recorder is good enough to make professional videos. The bar isn't very high, because you need to compress the videos so they can be downloaded. This will change.

Somebody brought up the story of a young marketer, who was a broke student who lived in Singapore. He e-mailed a bunch of gurus and asked them a simple question about marketing. He knew that getting an answer to an e-mail was easier than any other form of gathering information.

He also figured out that the gurus he interviewed would be emotionally involved with the product, and would be motivated to see it succeed. When the product was ready to market, his interview subjects became his joint-venture partners.

He made a pile of money.

This is a great business model. Joe and I used it when we created *The Myth of Passive Income*.

We attracted 23 successful authors and marketers to write a chapter. Then, when the e-book was ready to market, we asked our co-authors to be our joint-venture partners. Many of them did. The book is still selling.

YOUR E-BOOK BUSINESS FOR LESS THAN $100

O ne of the things I love about Internet marketing is the relationships I have with people all over the globe. It's a lot like traveling, but I get to stay in sunny Texas and "talk" to subscribers and customers who are shoveling snow in Michigan, sitting around a wood stove in the Black Forest of Germany, or braving the wind and rain in London.

I'm fascinated by the various ways that people live—aren't you?

If Wimberley, Texas, were to be hit by a major snowstorm that required shoveling snow, it would be a major disaster. We can't drive on ice. We don't know how and our cars aren't "set up" for it. Half an inch of snow is sufficient excuse to shut down the schools.

And yet, in much of the world, winter is just another season. People shovel snow, scrape ice from their windshields, check their snow tires, and go about their day.

Recently I received an e-mail from another Texan. His question sort of surprised me: "How much money should I put aside for my e-book business?"

My strategy is to identify a need or find a way to solve a problem, then package that solution and sell it. I write e-books, I record audio courses, and lately I've been making video courses. But I did have an answer to his question. He found the information valuable—maybe you will, too.

HOW MUCH MONEY DO YOU NEED
TO START YOUR E-BOOK BUSINESS?

I started mine with less than $100. First, you need an e-book. Some people make this way too big a deal. Remember, most people are "newbies." If you had to learn something, odds are somebody else is having to learn it, too. Write about what you learn.

You can write a list—for example, 69 ways to satisfy your husband, or 144 ways to cook spinach, or 37 Internet predictions.

"How to" books are easy, too. I like to learn something new, and then "hammer home" that new knowledge by writing an e-book to teach it to others. Teaching is a great way to learn.

Interview books are quick and painless. Call somebody on the phone and interview them. Record the call. Have it transcribed. Bim-bang-boom, you've got an e-book.

Get the idea?

Next, you need a web site. I use Microsoft Frontpage to build mine. If that's not your thing, go to www.elance.com and let the starving Web guys bid on the project. Should cost less than $50.

According to many pros, even if you can build a web site yourself, you're better off outsourcing that and concentrating on creating products. That's a lesson I'm still trying to learn.

You need a domain. Go to www.godaddy.com and buy one. They're about $8.

I collect domains. I own over 300 now, and I'm still shopping. Every time I think of (or overhear) a great domain name, I run to godaddy.com and register it.

When the time comes to market a new product, I go over my inventory of domains. Usually I have the perfect domain already registered. Then I just forward that to my sales page, no hosting fee.

You need a Clickbank account. That's gonna run you $50 (www.click bank.com).

It takes a little time to learn how to use Clickbank, but it's worth it. They handle the cash, send out affiliate checks when other people sell your e-book, and mail you your money twice a month. It's a bargain.

At that point, you've got a product, a sales page, and a way to collect the money and handle your affiliates.

The next step is to make money.

The most attractive way to do that is to do a joint-venture with somebody who has a huge list. The easiest way to do that is to have a relationship with one of the gurus. They're real human beings, and relatively harmless. Get to know them.

How do you get to know them? Seminars are the best way. E-mail works, too.

Every guru I know at least glances at every JV offer he gets. Some of the busier ones have a staff member go through them first.

If you can build a relationship before you make your joint-venture offer, you have a much better chance of connecting with your offer. Find out what your target guru is interested in—find some common ground—and start with that.

I certainly read all of the offers I get. You never know when that million-dollar idea is gonna land in your in-box.

If you've done all of the above, you've got an e-book business.

Congratulations.

THE SHORT COURSE ON INTERNET MARKETING

S tep into my office. I'm at the Ruta Maya Coffee Shop on South Congress Avenue in Austin, Texas.

It's hot, but we've got coffee, cigars, lots of water, and an interesting world to look at.

Now, let's talk about why some people are running successful Internet marketing businesses and some people are just talking about it.

If you've read this far, you know I have very strong opinions about what you need and what you don't need to run a successful business online.

You need: (1) a list, (2) a way to attract people to that list, and (3) products to sell to the people on that list.

In my opinion, that's all you need in the way of tools. The big work is to be done on the inside: getting your head straight about who you are, what you want, and getting comfortable with the fact that you live in an infinite universe and can have anything you want. If you'll let yourself.

So, outside your head, you need a list and products. You need to establish a relationship with that list. Let them get to know you and trust you. Don't offer them crappy products just to make a quick commission. Automate everything that can possibly be automated.

Once you've got that established, you can start looking for other people (affiliates) who can sell your products for you.

There are some other things that are, in my opinion, distractions. You can spend a fortune and a lifetime on the distractions. But if you focus on your list and your products you can build a business, and build it fast.

I know. It sounds too simple. That must be why some people try to make it so darn hard. You can make it hard if you want to, but it's really quite simple, and if it's hard—well, Joe Vitale talks about the escalator up the mountain of life. There is one. Some people enjoy the climb. They ignore the escalator, and scramble up the rocks. It takes longer, and is much harder, but if you want to take the long way—as long as you're choosing it with your eyes wide open—go for it.

However, if you want to jump on the escalator and zoom to the top, you need good information.

I've had the benefit of being able to hang out with some of the best: Dr. Vitale, Craig Perrine, Bill Hibbler, and others.

They'll let me get lost in the rocks for a while, but when I get tired of skinning my knees and breathing hard, I can count on them to pull me back to the escalator.

(The sun wins—it's too hot in Texas to sit outside drinking coffee and smokin' cigars. I'm gonna head out in search of the perfect taco.)

Do It!

From working with my mentoring clients, I've discovered that the "do it" part is the hard part. Like me, they have lots of unopened e-books on their hard drive.

Some of them are hesitant to launch products because they're unsure that they have anything of value to offer. I glaze right over this one, myself. I visualize a constantly moving parade. I joined the parade at the very back, but the minute I took my first step on the parade route, others joined behind me. Each step I take is a lesson I can teach to those behind me.

The more steps I take, the more people there are behind me to market to.

It's a mistake—and I've watched it totally freeze people—to worry about what those ahead of you in the parade will think of your products.

For example, it's unlikely that I'm going to teach Armand Morin much about Internet marketing. He's years ahead of me, has a large staff and a virtually unlimited budget.

Okay. I don't get that sale.

However, all of the people who have become curious about Internet marketing, and owning a home business you can operate from any Internet cafe in the galaxy, in the last two and a half years—those are sales I can make. And it's possible that because just two and half years ago I was in the back of the parade, I'm more qualified to teach to the beginning marketer than Armand is. The territory between there and here is very familiar to me. It's fresh in my mind; I remember clearly not knowing how to create a PDF file. I remember wrestling with 1shoppingcart, trying to set up my first autoresponder. I know how I went from "broke," to owning a successful business. I can teach that.

One of my clients asked me what a typical day is like for a successful Internet marketer. Well, my days are different from Joe's days, which are different from Bill's days, which are different from Craig's days, but there's one thing we all have in common: *action.*

At the risk of sounding like a TV commercial—we just do it.

What do we do? Here's what I do. If I were to have to wake up every morning, go to the same place, and do the same thing every day, I would quietly go crazy. I'm basically unemployable. I've had "real" jobs, and I've uniformly hated them.

So, for me, each day is different. I'm easily amused and easily distracted.

I tend to work late at night, after the rest of the family is asleep. That's probably a result of being a musician for so many years. Sometimes the first show doesn't start till 10 o'clock, or later. I've watched the sun come up over Austin, and Berlin, and Amsterdam, enough times to think it's perfectly normal when the sun comes up outside my office window.

Consequently, my mornings are slow. I wake up when I wake up. Starbucks French roast. Vitamins and supplements. E-mail. Check on my mentoring clients—they've all got private forums, where I can watch their progress.

I like to leave time to just sit and think. It's best to do this when nobody's around, because it looks like I'm daydreaming or brain damaged. I consider this to be the most valuable use of my time. When I'm in need of a project, that's when the ideas come. I used to do this while Betsy was at work and the kids were at school. Now that the kids are out of school and Betsy's off for the summer, I just do it when I do it. Sometimes I do it to Tool's new CD, which apparently sounds best at maximum volume. Patrick thinks so.

I can dig it. Layla sounded best that way, too.

The afternoons are when I do the "grunt" work. Format e-books, make MP3s from audio files, duplicate CDs, and so on. Boring, but it has to be done. Recently, I've hired a part-time employee to do some of this.

I tend to be project oriented. I like to visualize a project, start it, and finish it. Then take a break. Rinse and repeat.

Right now, I've got projects lined up for months, and I'm not sure I like it that way. I prefer to improvise. However, there are more seminars to promote. Hundreds of hours of video to shoot and edit. Joe had a great idea based on his manifestation weekend that I want to get to quickly. There's this book that I've been meaning to write—oh, I must have gotten that one done. You're holding it.

I try to not do two similar projects in a row. The only thing my projects will have in common is that I think they'll generate passive income, and I'll think they'll be fun. As I finish each one, it takes its place online. The income from that project joins the income from all the others, and is funneled into my bank account.

I like to choose projects that will continue to generate income long after I'm through with them. It's a real treat to look in my in-box, and see a sales e-mail for a product that I made two years ago. That's the truth about passive income. It's usually the result of massive action.

Some products are created and marketed quickly. Some projects take months. Sometimes the projects are obvious, and sometimes they're chosen based on what I think it would be fun to do. Sometimes they fall completely out of the blue. The essential next thing is to take action. When an idea shows up, move on it.

The real trick is realizing that *everything* is a product. Betsy and I are leaving for a quick minivacation this week. I'll take the little video camera and my digital SLR. From the road, I'll post pictures and stories that illustrate my Portable Empire. I suspect that I'll come up with a project idea or two. If so, I've got my laptop computer with me. I can edit video and still pictures, record audio, edit videos, and write.

Every time I learn something, I use it to make products. Some examples: learning to write e-books, learning to make video, learning to write copy. In Internet marketing, you can monetize your learning curve.

If you look at my previous blog postings, you'll see videos. The early ones suck. They gradually get better. What you're seeing is my learning curve. When you see the videos of the Unseminar—which are stunning— you'll see the result of all those hours of learning about video.

The real secret is I used my learning curve to drive traffic to my blog, and make money. I didn't worry about what the more experienced videographers would think of my videos. That's irrelevant. What was important to me was: (1) creating something of value that would interest my subscribers and (2) learning to make better videos.

Putting on the Unseminar was the biggest project I'd ever undertaken at the time. It would have been nice to have some downtime after that, but I had to deal with the videos and audios. They needed to be edited.

That led to the next obvious project: editing the videos and audios.

After I finished editing the audios and videos from the Unseminar, I delivered the masters to the duplication/shipping people (the fulfillment house). When the orders started coming in, these are the people who make the DVDs and CDs, put them in a box, and ship them.

To get the project to this point, I had to learn how to edit video and then edit about 30 hours of video. It was fun. Learning how to create titles that draw the viewer into the screen and put him/her in the room at the Unseminar. How to compress the audio tracks, and mix in the music, to make it sound great. How to take out the unnecessary stuff, without leaving holes and keep the continuity flowing.

It was a simple matter of putting one foot in front of the other and being patient with myself. It required a lot of 16-hour days.

Of course, when we sold over $100,000 of the videos last July, it took some of the sting out of all that work. It ain't passive income, but it ain't bad. And it's nothing you can't do. Over time, it becomes passive income. We'll be selling those videos for years.

My strategy is to visualize it. Just build it in my mind, and then look at the outcome. Once I've completely visualized the successful experience, it's easy to make it appear in the real world.

WHAT DOES ALL THIS MEAN TO YOU?

How do you use this info to make money?

Your mission, should you choose to accept it, is to create multiple streams of passive income that you can create and maintain from anywhere on the planet that has Internet access. That's how you get your own Portable Empire. Take action. Now. Do it. Don't worry about—anything. Negative predictions, catastrophising, fear of failure, fear of success—worry about that later.

One step at a time.

This is done by creating the first stream of passive income. This can be as simple as creating a workbook from a public domain book and putting it on Clickbank.

It's unlikely that you'll be able to live off the first one. So—rinse and repeat—create your second stream of passive income. Maybe you could interview your auto mechanic on how to increase gas mileage. Put that online.

That's a start.

After a while, you'll realize that you're not just working to "live." The rent or mortgage is paid, the car payment is paid, and you keep working because you enjoy the game. Big houses and cars are there if you want them, but that's not why you're working.

It's really quite simple, but it requires you to take some action. It requires you to do something to build your Portable Empire every day.

One day, you'll wake up, turn on your computer, check your e-mail, check your bank balance, and just grin. It is a wonderful feeling.

GOLD ON THE PLAYGROUND

If It's Hard, You're Doing It Wrong

> **If it's work, it won't make you rich.**
>
> —Dan Kennedy

> **If it ain't fun, I ain't doin' it.**
>
> —Pat O'Bryan, May 1996

At a recent Mastermind meeting, the joke was on me. We were talking about projects I have in progress, and Bill said, "He'll probably have 'em done before sundown."

Joe, Craig, and Nerissa laughed—and, I think, in a nice way.

I've gotten a reputation as the guy who cranks out dozens of products while others are still talking and planning theirs.

Here's another good quote:

> **Money loves speed.**
>
> —Joe Vitale

The secret to making a good living from infoproduct marketing is having multiple streams of passive income. Yes, some people make a million bucks in one day. Some gurus have five- and six-figure days consistently. Home runs are nice, but you can build a very solid business with a string of base hits.

Find a problem and sell the solution. Then find another one. Do this enough times, and you've got multiple streams of passive income.

Each of us has a reason why we build our Portable Empire. Some people come from a place of fear. It can be a risky world. Which is riskier: a steady job with a steady paycheck or a Portable Empire? You don't have to choose, by the way, but it's an interesting mental exercise.

There are lots of ways you can lose a job. The job can be outsourced to another country. The company can be bought, and the job "downsized." You can have a "personality conflict" with your boss. Your boss's girlfriend may need a job, and yours might be it.

With a steady job with a steady paycheck, you're guaranteed to make less than you're worth, by definition. The difference between what they pay you and what you're worth is called "profit," and if the company doesn't make a profit, your boss might lose his job. Whose job do you think is more important to your boss—yours or his?

With a Portable Empire, you have multiple streams of passive income. One by one, you build up steady, repeatable, and sustainable streams of income that you control. Contrary to conventional wisdom, that seems the safest, most conservative path.

My "reason why" is fun. I choose my projects based on how much fun I think they'll be. In my case, I create and market audio products for "inner-directed professionals" at www.instantchange.com. I've taught hundreds of new business owners how to create their own Portable Empires. I write and co-write e-books on various subjects.

I've been a musician since I was a small child. I really can't help it. I'm addicted to that magic process, and the moment when I hit "play" in the recording studio and listen to a piece of music that I've written and recorded is payday for me. The fact that I can sell that audio product is just gravy. Mostly.

I love to write. I come from a long line of writers. My father was a professional writer. He and two of my uncles were newspaper publishers. I can remember going to bed as a child to the music of my father's type-writer clacking in the next room.

And that moment when I convert my latest e-book to a PDF and it appears on the screen as a finished, professional product is also magic. It's a way in which we exist in God's image. The act of creation is one of the most spiritual things we, as mere humans, can do. The fact that the income from those e-books supports my lifestyle is just gravy. Mostly.

I love coaching. It may be the "big brother" in me, although, looking back, I'd like another shot at being a big brother. Like parenting, it's something I think I could do better the second time around.

It may also be a genetic predisposition. Both of my siblings, several of my cousins, and at least two aunts and one uncle are all educational professionals. It runs in the family.

I could never operate in the public school environment. My mind processes public schools as prisons. I'm eternally grateful that my son was comfortable in charter schools and is now out of school. From the design of the buildings to the attitude of the administration, I found lots to rebel against in the public school environment. No fun there for me.

But I do love to teach. I especially love to teach students who love to learn. My students must love to learn—I charge them for it, and I'm expensive. I'm a pretty tough teacher. By focusing on fun, I've created a teaching environment that pays much better than teaching in the public schools. Just gravy. Sort of. (I'm about to make a startling confession.)

I'm also addicted to the thrill of watching invoices slam my in-box.

There. I've admitted it.

I do love the process of creating. But I also love the thrill of the hunt. Creating something and then finding that it resonates with others—enough so that they will part with their hard-earned cash to purchase it—is akin to the feeling that some bow hunters must feel after they've spent hours or days tracking an elusive elk, and have subdued it.

It's fun.

It's especially fun when it happens fast. Those times when I've gone from concept to cash in a day or so—when the rush is on, and I'm focused and in the zone—are times I relish. It's when I'm at my best.

There are those who choose their projects based on time-intensive research and planning. Scouring Google and Overture to find out what the hot search subjects are and then creating products based on their research.

I don't think I could get passionate about a subject that way, although I do research my own way. I hang out on forums—usually at www.your portableempire.com—and see what questions are being asked. Those questions represent a problem that somebody is having. I love to solve problems. I just hang out and see which problems resonate with me. What solution would be fun to come up with?

I love the puzzles that the infomarketing game presents. I have a saying, "Every problem is a product." That's how the whole *Absolute Beginner's Guide . . .* series got started. I figured that if I was having trouble with something, others would be, too. I was right. A niche was born, and now I'm the author of a series of books on solutions for Absolute Beginners and a recognized expert in the field.

It's pretty amazing what you can accomplish if you focus on fun.

Now, I'm exploring video and the ways it can be utilized to solve problems. I'm able to visualize several applications, from straight-ahead educational videos to psychological conditioning training.

I stumbled on this niche totally by accident. I just thought it might be fun to have a video camera to record my first Unseminar. It was fun. That seminar was in May 2006. In July 2006, we released the videos of that seminar and grossed well over $100,000 in sales.

Now I've got three video cameras, and a state-of-the-art video editing suite.

The world is full of experts and interesting people. Making a video of them is a quick and easy way to create products. Who knew?

What's this got to do with Internet marketing and, more importantly, what's this got to do with you?

If you're wondering how to create your own online empire, let me tell you the secret. Look at all the possibilities. Imagine what you would do if you had no fear, and no limitations. Then, holding those options in your mind, let yourself feel each one—and find the ones that feel like fun.

That's where you want to play. That's your playground. And, proving once again that the universe is a wonderful, magical, holodeck of a place, that's where you'll find your success.

Million Dollar Questions

Yesterday I was participating in a conversation, and a woman said, "I stayed in bed all day. The house was such a mess that I just couldn't face it."

How did the house get in such a mess? Did gremlins sneak in and trash her house? Did small children crawl out from behind her furniture when she wasn't looking and make messes?

Somebody else asked her, "Have you considered just cleaning your house?"

She looked at them with wide-eyed amazement. It hadn't occurred to her that she could actually clean up the mess she had made, and thereby allow herself to get out of her bed and actually live her life.

What does this story have to do with you?

TRANCES, EVIL MAGICIANS—AND THE COUNTER-SPELL

One of the secrets that all hypnotists, and hypnotic writers, know is that we're all in a trance. Hypnotic writers try to anticipate their reader's trance state and meet them there, and then lead them placidly to the "buy now" button.

Once you start looking for it, the signs are everywhere. It's much easier to see in others than it is to see in ourselves, and that's a start.

The most important thing you can do—and I mean this in a macrosense—like the most important thing you can do for yourself, right now, in your life—is to wake up. It's that simple.

How do you wake up? I find it useful to question every thing. Every Thing. A healthy curiosity may just save your life.

In my case, I was in a trance about my weight. I'd look in the mirror to shave, brush my hair, and so on, and never even notice the bulge that kept making my shirts harder and harder to button. It was as if a magician had waved a wand and put me under a spell.

It's even harder than that, though. You're under attack. There are armies of highly professional, talented magicians who are casting spells—and they're aiming them at you.

Every TV commercial you see, every word out of every politician's mouth, over 80 percent of what you read in newspapers, is carefully scripted by these magicians—and they do not have your best interests at heart. They do have their hands in your pocket, though.

How can you protect yourself from these armies of evil magicians?

Simple.

There are two rules that I have found that will keep you relatively trance free.

1. Thou shalt not b.s. thyself. You are as rich, smart, fat or thin, as you really are. Once you realize your true condition, then you can take action to change it if you don't like it.

   If you're b.s.ing yourself, you'll never make the changes. And after a while, you won't even trust yourself. Down this path lies madness, and dangerous weight gain, in my case.
2. Wake up. Question everything you hear. After a while, this will become second nature. Initially, you'll have to consciously practice being awake.

Now, you are feeling sleepy. Your eyes are heavy. I don't know when, but soon you're going to return to your trance and send $1,000 to Pat's Paypal account.

EVIL MAGICIANS

Who are the *Evil Magicians*? They are the ones who use the psychology of persuasion to cause you to do things that are not in your best interest.

For example, when you see an athlete promoting an automobile, you're seeing a psychological principle in operation. In your mind, you may already have a relationship with the athlete. If he tells you to buy a certain automobile, he sets up a quandary for you: To retain your relationship with the athlete, you have to believe what he says. If you use your critical thinking ability to question what he's saying, you run the risk of losing your relationship with the athlete—and you value that relationship.

Now, the relationship is all in your mind—but so is the entire universe. Your perception of the world is the only real world you've got.

You don't want to lose your relationship with that athlete—he's your athlete. You cheer for him when he plays inside your television. You feel good when he wins. You feel sad when he loses.

He's never heard of you, by the way. Again, the Evil Magicians are using their magic to take advantage of your trance. Really, in what way does aptitude with the hoops prepare an athlete to be an expert on automobiles?

If you're feeling a little superior—you don't pay any attention to athletes—remember that this trick will work with any hero. One of my favorite artists, Peter Max, did a commercial for a credit card company. Many actors, authors, playwrights, and other "heroes" augment their income by shilling for products.

THE COUNTER-SPELL

Do you know who people buy from?

> People they like.
> Who do people like?
> People like them.

That's another psychological principle called, oddly enough, the principle of "liking."

Check out the soft drink commercials. Look at how the actors are dressed and how they talk. There is usually a group of them, and they're carefully wardrobed and coached to appeal to a segment of the market.

The Evil Magicians are trying to get you to put yourself in their picture.

Watch the car commercials—but outside of your trance. Notice how the family cars are advertised with families, sports cars are advertised using actors who look young, and single.

They're trying to catch you in your trance and get you to put yourself in the picture, which will cause a feeling of discomfort until you actually buy the product to complete the picture.

What weapon can you possibly use against the highly trained, highly paid, Evil Magicians that are casting spells on you from all sides?

What can you use to draw a circle of white light around yourself, to ward off the psychological tricksters who are trying to use your trance to take your money?

Knowledge.

That and a healthy sense of curiosity.

Dr. Milton Erickson was the original wizard, who came up with most of the psychological tricks that advertisers are using today. Bandler and

Grinder, the guys who started neurolinguistic programming (NLP) were a couple of his students. There have been others who have built on his work, including me.

To learn how to recognize psychological operations (psy-ops) when they're aimed at you, by advertisers, wingnuts, politicians, you're going to have to do a little homework. It will be the most rewarding homework you ever do, because once you learn to recognize these nasty little tricks, you're immune.

You might even use them yourself.

To learn all about counter—spells, go to www.influence101.com.

Zen and the Art of Internet Marketing

Want to hear something wild? I've discovered the most fascinating thing: At the top level, where the really successful Internet marketers seem to effortlessly acquire money, success, and power, there is quite an interest in Oriental philosophy.

Oriental philosophy, specifically early Tao and Zen writings, has been my secret weapon since my early college days. I don't talk about it much, but when it comes to focusing on the task at hand, being completely "in the moment," and creating products at light speed, the techniques I've learned from Tao and Zen writers never let me down.

I'm talking about Tao and Zen as taught up to about the fourth century A.D., when they were philosophies and their writings were just collections of intelligent ways to operate in the universe.

Around that time, somebody had the bright idea of turning the philosophies into religions, an idea that would have amused Lao Tsu, for example, the guy who started Taoism. They get a little boring after that.

Imagine my surprise when I started recognizing the same techniques, with a different spin, coming at me from the marketing and wealth-building books I've been reading!

The Power of Impossible Thinking is a great example. It explains how your belief systems are choices, and how you can choose to change them. It's brilliant, once you learn the trick. You can choose specific belief systems that are task-appropriate, without becoming attached to them.

That's right out of the Tao te Ching!

Another example: *177 Mental Toughness Secrets of the World Class*, by Steve Siebold. It lists 177 traits of world class successes, and guess what? They're pretty much the same traits Taoists and Zen practitioners were teaching several thousand years ago!

You may think I've lost my mind, but in reality, whatever that is—here, let me give you an example:

"The World Class Raises Their Rate of Vibration at Will" is the title of one of the chapters in Siebold's book. He's just reframed an ancient meditation technique and packaged it for businessmen. I love this!!

What they all agree on is the importance of "now." This moment. We live in a series of "nows."

> You can be happy now.
>
> You can be successful now.
>
> And now is the only time you can be happy or successful.

Now is also the only time you can actually accomplish anything.

ON THE BACK ROADS WITH A PORTABLE EMPIRE

Colin Joss

In late November 2006 I launched my first e-book, Inspired Attraction, on an unsuspecting public.

For most of the first day, I sat at my laptop computer, clicking the refresh button every couple of minutes, waiting for the sales to roll in.

And surprisingly they did. By the end of the first day, I'd earned $154.54. By the end of the first week, I'd earned $2,129.70. And by the end of the first month, I'd earned a jaw dropping $5,926.09.

I had a grin to beat the Cheshire Cat.

Less than a year earlier I was struggling in a nine-to-five hell, living for the weekends and family vacations. If success was a journey, I was broken down on the side of the highway.

But now, with Internet marketing, I'd discovered a back road to financial freedom and peace of mind.

Like most people I'd tried to make my fortune on the Internet before. I'd heard the runaway success stories of Google and Lastminute.com. All I needed was a million dollar idea and a hot web site.

But after the fourth or fifth web site failed, I abandoned the sites like junked cars at the side of the highway.

After that, I read there was money to be made with online auctions. I bought a trinket from a local store and listed it on eBay. And it sold.

With the profit, I bought a couple more trinkets and listed them. Both failed to sell. By that time, however, the thought of a spare room crammed with products and endless trips to the post office killed my desire for an eBay fortune.

But the dream of walking out of my dead-end job and making a living sitting in my pajamas still haunted me. It continued to haunt me until the summer of 2005.

On a family vacation in Florida, I discovered Joe Vitale's *The Attractor Factor* in the local Barnes & Noble. Of course Joe's five easy steps for creating wealth inspired me. But his stories of Internet marketing, of writing e-books and selling them online, inspired me more.

In that one book I discovered a potential escape route from the nine-to-five grind. I began to imagine living the lifestyle of a successful Internet marketer.

- I imagined waking each morning, stumbling sleepily to my home office, checking my e-mail and discovering I'd made hundreds of dollars overnight.
- I imagined sitting in Starbucks, writing my latest e-book while sipping a chai tea latte.

Back home, after the vacation, I signed up for Joe's newsletter. With each e-mail, my hunger for Internet marketing grew.

I bought my first product on writing e-books from Joe. I read it but I didn't put it into action. It simply sat on my hard drive.

I bought another product. And another. And another. Each one packed with quality information but I refused to use it. For some reason I was sabotaging myself.

I knew I needed to give myself a swift kick up the backside. But I didn't know how.

On April 18, 2006, the answer came in an e-mail from Pat O'Bryan. In the e-mail, Pat announced his No B.S. mentoring program. I sat and read that e-mail a dozen times or more before I signed up.

With Pat's endless support, during the next couple of months I created a collection of e-books from the public domain and gave them away at www.trowardcollection.com to build a list of over 600 subscribers almost overnight.

A month after that I sent out an e-mail to a number of outrageously successful people asking them to write a contribution for my next e-book. I wanted to know how they used the law of attraction in their day-to-day lives.

Eventually, 12 people responded and, along with my own contribution, I created Inspired Attraction—available at www.inspiredattraction.com.

With Inspired Attraction I'd created my first stream of passive income. Each day I make at least one sale—often many more.

It's now early January 2007. In a couple of weeks, I'm launching another information product called Applied Psychology. It's a series of 12 books on success in life and business, originally published in 1914. When people invest in it—at www.appliedpsychologyonline.com—it becomes another stream of passive income.

With some of the money I've earned, I've hired a web designer to redesign my web site at www.colinjoss.com and to create me some really cool logos for T-shirts, baseball caps, and coffee mugs.

In just over a month, I'm heading to Texas to attend Pat O'Bryan's Unseminar 3. I'll meet Pat and Joe and the rest of the Wimberley Hole-in-the-Wallet gang. It's mind-blowing to think that I'll be in the same room as these guys.

But the web sites, the seminars, and the streams of passive income are only symbols of success. To get up in the morning with a passion for the day ahead, to live that day as you darn well please, and to go to bed at night knowing you've lived the best day possible is real success.

I'm not quite there yet but I'm on my way.

Colin Joss is the founder of Back Roads Marketing. You can subscribe to his free monthly On the Back Roads newsletter at www.colinjoss.com.

MARNA'S STORY

Six months ago I was working as vice president of marketing for a local hospice making between $60,000 and $80,000, depending on bonuses, which are taxed at 40 percent. Really, I was bringing home, after taxes, around $35,000 to $45,000.

Six wonderful months ago, I decided to quit my job and work full-time on my business, thinwithin.com. While I'm writing this, it's 10:30 A.M. and I'm still sitting in bed with my pajamas on absolutely loving life. I have four new partnerships in the works, I'm far surpassing the amount of money I was bringing in before, and I have time to do the things I love and be with people I care about. I am also full of possibilities, life, and energy. The stress in my life and my body have totally vanished.

Further, I did attend Pat's Unseminar 2 and I kid you not, the very next month, thinwithin.com doubled the amount of money it brought in from the month prior.

After I quit my job, I was tempted to follow up on other vice president or director job opportunities that colleagues told me about. Now, I would never think of it! This is the life. It's miraculous. Every day I wake up so grateful to have the clients, the partnerships, and the opportunities I have.

Thanks to incredible people like Pat, you can do what I've done: live your dreams!

Thank you, Pat.

Marna Goldstein
Owner of www.thinwithin.com

PART TWO

MIND-SET OF SUCCESS

YOUR INNER GAME

Knowing "how to" set up and run your Portable Empire is only half the battle.

Yes, the nuts and bolts skills of list building, copywriting, product creation, and relationship marketing are all important. You need these skills.

However, I think the "mindset of success" skills are even more important.

The Internet marketing universe is densely populated with people who know "how to," and still aren't successful.

I've never met anyone who had their inner game together who wasn't successful.

For example, my friend Joe Vitale doesn't have a clue how to design a web page and put it online. Cindy Cashman is even less interested in the technical aspects of internet marketing than Joe.

They've both made millions of dollars. They seem to magically attract what they need.

I've asked Cindy how she comes up with answers and inspiration. She says, "PFA!"

"What's PFA?"

"Pluck From Air," she says. Then she giggles. She makes it look easy, because, to her, it is easy. She doesn't need to know "how to." She's living the mind-set of success.

This mind-set is a little more challenging to teach, because each person starts from where they are, with their own beliefs, filters, and preconceptions.

The following chapters contain hints and clues. I've included stories with examples of how I've grown and learned to use my inner game to improve my business.

To further explore your inner game, I recommend that you get a copy of *The Attractor Factor,* by Dr. Joe Vitale, and read it. And live it. Joe's new book, *Zero Limits,* is an even deeper look into the subject. You can find them at Amazon.com.

The movie, *The Secret,* is another great resource. You can get it www.thesecret.tv.

These resources will lead you to others. It's a fun journey. It may also be the most profitable journey you ever embark on.

FEEDING YOURSELF

The phrase "feeding yourself" kind of follows Maslow's hierarchy, doesn't it?

When you're broke, feeding yourself means finding enough food.

Later, it might be more about choosing between caviar and truffles.

After you get enough toys and truffles, you start to bump into those tricky "self-actualization" issues.

Picture this: In Zen mythology there is a character who figured it out. He was probably born into royalty, although nobody's really sure. He achieved material success and turned his back on it. He lived in the hills, enjoyed good wine, and got a kick out of making fun of the serious monks.

He figured out that we already live in the garden, and he made the most of it. Come to think of it, most pictures and statues of Buddha picture him smiling, don't they?

A careful reading of the world's spiritual texts—the ones that absolutely resonate with the crystal inevitability of truth-turn up no references to material possessions as the path to happiness. And yet, what do we spend our time on?

Why?

Listen to Yo-Yo Ma, the cellist, when he talks about playing his cello. Even after decades of playing the cello, his most treasured moments are the ones when he sits alone, caressing his cello and drawing transcendent music from it.

When he talks about his instrument, and his relationship with it, you can feel the rich, centuries-old wood, see the deep grain, and hear the timeless tone as his bow brings the strings and wood to life. He loves what he does.

He doesn't care if he's alone or in front of thousands; he's feeding his soul by playing his cello.

He's also become stunningly wealthy, but he didn't get rich by focusing on money.

I get the same feeling from the Internet marketing gurus I've met—the ones who have gone to the stratosphere of marketing. They're not focusing on money. They've got bags of the stuff.

I think that's why Joe Vitale's Spiritual Marketing philosophy feels so right to me. I can testify that you can make piles of money following his marketing strategies, but I can also testify that making money is the byproduct of the process, not the goal.

When you listen to the real superstars in marketing, you realize quickly that their goals are not strictly about themselves. Yeah, they arrive in nice cars and go home to nice houses, but that's not their focus.

Joe's seminar in Austin, January 2004, was my introduction to the world of marketing, and I quickly realized a couple of things:

1. If you diligently follow the strategies of almost *any* of the speakers, you will make a consistent income.
2. The really successful speakers were happy to teach you how to make money, but what they wanted to talk about was the way they were making the world a better place with their money. One speaker goes to poor villages in Mexico and provides medicine and medical care. Another funds a foundation that provides scholarships to bright kids who can't afford college. Another works with economically challenged young athletes. They were feeding themselves by feeding others.

The general consensus was that the more they gave, the more they got—financially and spiritually. They also seemed to be having a lot of fun, which is hard to do if you narrow your focus to just enhancing your own financial position.

You can't outgive the universe. The more you give, the more you get.

How are you going to make the world a better place while you're feeding yourself?

YOUR MONEY THERMOSTAT

What's your "money thermostat" set to? Interesting question, huh?

At a recent mastermind meeting, Dr. Joe Vitale passed out copies of *"Secrets of the Millionaire Mind"* by T. Harv Eker. It's really making me look at my beliefs about money.

Ol' T. Harv makes the case that everybody has a money thermostat that governs how much money we allow ourselves to make. It's something we learn from our parents, usually.

There are other internal thermostats: happiness thermostats, health and weight thermostats, relationship thermostats.

The bad news is that we're pretty much a bundle of conditioned responses. According to Napoleon Hill, and I've seen no data that refutes this, by the time we're fifteen, we're programmed. Unless we make a conscious effort to intelligently reprogram ourselves, we're stuck with the beliefs, conditioning, and thermostats that we're given as children.

The good news is that we *can* reprogram ourselves. This is something I've been working on for quite a while. My money thermostat was set at about whatever my bills for each month happened to be. I used to be pretty smug about the fact that the universe took such good care of me.

The problem was that I could never get ahead. If I needed a few hundred bucks to pay a bill, it would (apparently) appear out of nowhere, but not a penny more. I was stuck.

Looking back, I can reverse engineer this phenomenon. My dad was the same way. His dad was the same way. It's learned behavior.

I decided to "unlearn" it. I had some added baggage. I'm an old hippie. There. I admit it. There's a lot about the counterculture I still embrace, mostly ecological and social issues.

It can be very conflicting.

- Part of me would be perfectly happy in a Buddhist monastery, with my personal material wealth consisting of a bowl, a saffron robe, and a library card.
- Another part of me wants that Mercedes-Benz and a villa in northern Italy.

What finally turned me around was the discovery that we live in an infinite universe. The universe has unlimited wealth. I can reprogram my internal thermostats to allow any amount of money, happiness, and bliss I want.

That changes everything. Just by changing my internal beliefs about money, I've managed to increase my income by an order of magnitude in less than a year.

Take a look at your thermostats. How much money have you allowed yourself to make? How much happiness have you allowed yourself to have?

It's all up to you, you know.

SELF-SABOTAGE SOLUTION

At another mastermind Meeting, when it was my turn to talk about my week, I thought I could get away with not mentioning the fact that I poured about eight ounces of Shiraz/Cabernet into my laptop computer the previous Tuesday.

Wrong.

I had already talked about how I had written a new e-book between supper and bedtime this Tuesday, redesigned the Milagro web site, my new coaching program, the new CD factory I'm putting together. I thought I was through. And then Bill said, "What about your mandatory vacation?"

As it so often does, telling the story at the mastermind meeting led me to some new realizations.

It's true that I knocked over a glass of wine into my laptop computer. I already knew that. This very effectively put me out of business. I run all of my projects—from my audio and video projects to my web pages to my e-books—from my laptop computer.

But what I found myself talking about was self-sabotage. That's been my pattern for decades. I'll have a little success, and then I'll blow it. I'll save a little money, and then do something that makes the money just disappear.

I know that I'm responsible for everything that happens in my life. I learned that recently, and it's one of the most important things I've ever learned. It's the undeniable truth.

And when I realized that I was self-sabotaging again, I literally grabbed my subconscious mind by the throat and told it, "Not this time." It was almost physical.

My neural pathways are so used to self-sabotage that it required a massive, conscious effort to change the behavior.

It's all part of being mindful. Making the right decisions moment to moment. And not lying to yourself.

It would make a better story if I could say that I accidentally knocked that glass over, wouldn't it?

That would be bs.

The truth is, I was achieving a level of success that exceeded where my success thermostat was set. My comfort level for success was programmed fairly low. Getting much above that level made me uncomfortable, so I did something (unconsciously) to bring me back into the comfort zone. The only way to maintain that new level of success is to reset my success thermostat.

Watching Joe reach his level of success, and live through it, is inspirational. Reading *The Millionaire Mind* helped, too.

It's going to take constant practice of mindfulness to do it, but I am resetting my success thermostat, moment by moment. In the same way a heroin addict doesn't do heroin. Moment by moment.

Oh yeah. My computer guy gave the laptop a serious and intrusive cleaning and ran the keyboard through his dishwasher. It works fine.

AUTHENTICITY

L et's talk about authenticity. One of the things I'm working with my clients on is being authentic. Have you noticed that some writers, especially on the Internet, put on their "internet marketing voice" when they write?

What's up with that? Their copy reads like they want you to know they put on a suit, tie, polished shoes, and clean underwear to write. I don't want to read that!

It reminds me of conversations I've had at Internet marketing seminars where otherwise normal people, with whom I was having a normal (and interesting) conversation, suddenly started talking about Internet marketing, and their whole vocabulary and affect changed completely.

When I curl up with a book—and lately it's been mostly Kinky Friedman, Christopher Moore, and Douglas Adams for fiction, and Joe Vitale and Dan Kennedy for nonfiction—what intrigues me, and keeps me reading, is the author's voice.

Dan Kennedy doesn't write like he's wearing a suit, and neither does Joe. They write like they talk, and I'll read them for hours.

Kinky Friedman writes like he's had one too many shots of Jameson's. Chris Moore writes like I would write if I was as talented as he is, and Douglas Adams wrote like an appalled visitor from another planet.

But the point is, each author has his own voice. They write as if they were sitting in your living room, sharing a cup of coffee, and telling you a story, or in Dan and Joe's case, telling you how to do something you really want to learn how to do.

Some of the e-books that hit my in-box just don't have an authentic voice, and it's a struggle to get through them.

Some successful authors dictate their articles and e-books and have them transcribed. One Internet marketer calls up a (patient) friend and tells them the article over the phone.

Whatever it takes is whatever it takes. If you want people to read what you write, write it in your authentic voice.

By the way, if this sounds like it was written by a guy in gym shorts with his feet up on his desk, and you're still reading, I succeeded!

THE GOLD ZONE

———

Betsy and I were just talking about the difference between how things feel when you're in the "gold zone" and how they feel when you're not.

Julia Cameron calls it the Vein of Gold and wrote a great book about it. Athletes call it the Zone. Let's call it the Gold Zone.

She was reminding me of the months right before I got serious about Internet marketing.

I had been a working musician since I was fifteen. I went "on the road" the first time when I was seventeen. I was gone for three months, and it was hard on me and hard on my family when I had to come back from being "on the road" to finish high school. I took several detours, but for the most part, I was a musician for over 30 years.

In spite of some success, I never really "made it" as a musician. I got really, really close a few times, but something would always go wrong.

For example, in 2003 I played an extended tour of Europe. We went to Sweden, Holland, France, and England. I played from Bogner Regis in the far south of England all the way up to the Isle of Aran in northern Scotland. It was a wonderful tour, and the people seemed to like my music.

The scenery was breathtaking. From Moose in Sweden to the Holy Isle in Scotland to the coffee shops in Amsterdam to the street performers in London.

Everything was wonderful except things kept going wrong. My bandmates made the decision to stay completely amphibious for the whole tour. Blame it on Amsterdam. The big festival in Sweden got no promotion, and almost nobody came. That's a long way to drive to play for 20 people.

And then I got robbed at Waverley Abbey, outside of London. Lost both guitars and all the money. And my passport.

I was clearly not in the Gold Zone.

After I finally got home—and believe me, with no money and no passport, getting home was tricky—I took some time off to think things through.

I had started researching the Internet marketing game, and had met some of the players. It was interesting, but there were a lot of unknowns. There were also some very steep (but relatively short) learning curves involved.

So, while I was thinking, my agents booked another tour, this time to Germany. That was the tour when all hell broke loose.

Betsy was alone with the boys, both of whom woke up one morning and decided to start acting like the teenagers they were. It was like fishing at the old pond, where the most dangerous thing you'd had to deal with was a catfish, and suddenly a 50-foot alligator jumps in the boat.

And I was over 3,000 miles away.

After that tour, I really did some thinking.

I either had to move to Europe and play music or do something else. Moving to Europe, at that time, just wasn't going to work. And more importantly, it just didn't feel right. Betsy and the boys also had strong opinions about that.

Worse, every time I strapped on my guitar, I felt like the "rock-star police" were going to arrest me. For impersonating a musician. I never once felt authentic as a musician.

This is odd. I was an award-winning songwriter, with a recording contract, zealous agents, and a publishing deal.

I was a fraud.

I know some real musicians. I have a guitar-player friend who has several gold records on his wall. He tours with a band that has had #1 singles. When he's home, he sits in his studio and plays guitar. For fun.

I once heard an interview with Yo-Yo Ma, and it really touched me. He talked about the most wonderful moments of his life. Those moments are when he takes his million dollar+ cello out of its case and sits alone, just loving the sound and touch of his instrument.

My guitars stay in their cases between tours. That was a clue.

Ever since I discovered Internet marketing, I've been in the Gold Zone. It was like finally seeing the PULL sign on a door I had been trying to push open for decades.

Duh.

It was crystal-clear to me.

I "got it" at the first Internet marketing seminar I attended. The people who were successful were the ones who made products and sold them. The people who were not successful were the ones who did something else, or did nothing.

I had a lot of help. I've immersed myself in Internet marketing, read scores of books, and sought out the company of successful internet marketers. I threw myself at learning curves, and bounded right up them.

I had a blast. I quickly made a pile of money. I found my Gold Zone.

Have you found your Gold Zone, yet?

It's easy, especially in the Internet marketing world. You can make a good, even a *great*, living by solving other people's problems. It pays well, and it's karmically good for you. You can pick almost any subject—cooking, driving, relationships, e-book authoring, and so on.

I have a saying that will eventually be turned into a book: "Every problem is a product."

My first book was *The Absolute Beginner's Guide to Internet Wealth*. It was easy to write. I just identified the five essential problems that Absolute Beginners to Internet marketing have and gave the solutions.

Thousands and thousands of people now have copies of that book. That's good for them, because the book really does line up all the problems and solutions that a new Internet marketer needs to know about.

It's good for me. I used that book to build a large and responsive list. I also get the psychic benefits of helping a lot of people. I like that.

So, I make money and I help others. Perfect niche.

How can you tell if you're in your Gold Zone? Things get real easy.

One of the things I stress to my coaching clients is, "If this is hard for you, you're doing it wrong."

If you find yourself getting bogged down and disinterested in your topic, you've picked the wrong topic. Quickly choose another one. If your subscribers consistently choose to not buy your products, quickly change your strategy. In the online world, you can make dramatic changes instantly.

Life is too short to bang your head against the door marked PULL. You can push and push and bang and hit and throw bombs and cry and just generally exhaust yourself. And the door will stay closed.

I would say that the most important thing you can do to improve your life is find your Gold Zone. Find your passion, and then find people to pay you for doing what you love.

Quit banging on the door and just open it.

How Big
Is Your Box?

L ast Monday I attended a birthday party for a musician/studio owner friend of mine. The party was held at a fairly rowdy honky-tonk in historic Gruene, Texas. There were bar-b-que, chips and hot sauce, and adult beverages. The focus of the party was a free-for-all jam session.

Who else but musicians get together and work for fun? I'm trying to imagine a bunch of accountants, getting together over bar-b-que and beer, with spreadsheets and green visors. For fun. Not gonna happen.

Back to the party. It was a blast, but I left early. As much fun as playing guitar can be, I felt the pull of my laptop. I had a couple of promotions going on, some coaching clients who needed help.

The Internet marketing game is addictive. I'm hooked. But I got an Internet marketing lesson between sets at the jam session. It was fascinating.

There was a guitar player there who was just amazing. Played rings around everybody else there. He sang like a country Otis Redding. He's a nice guy, trying to live like I used to live, playing bars in Texas for $30 to $50 a night.

I took him aside, and asked him if he'd like to break into the next level. I offered to introduce him to my European agents. I might as well have been talking to a brick.

His vision extends just about as far as the next bar gig. He's about as likely to fly to Europe and tour as he is to fly to the moon on a motorcycle. It ain't gonna happen.

Why?

Why can some musicians make the transition to recording artists and touring acts while others, who are just as talented, spend their lives playing bars for no money?

It's the size of their "box."

Bill Hibbler and I were talking about this today, and we realized that the same thing is true of Internet marketers.

Why do some Internet marketers just take off and build successful businesses, while others, who are just as talented, continue to struggle?

Bill's the one who said it. "It's the size of their box." Your world can be as big or as small as you let it be. That's your box. You can succeed as much as you let yourself succeed—that's your box, too.

You attract what you focus on. Focusing on concepts and objects that expand your box will make your world bigger.

I hang out in several Internet marketing forums, and run one, at www .yourportableempire.com. When I read threads posted by successful marketers, they're almost always positive in tone, and energetic. When I read threads by those who are struggling, they're almost always negative, limited, and dull.

My guitar playing buddy would do great in Europe. He's the perfect combination of blues and country. He just can't visualize doing it. He focuses on how hard it is to make it in the music business, how club owners don't want to pay very much for bands, how the audience doesn't appreciate his music. And that's what he attracts.

I laid it out for him in plain English, and he just couldn't see it. He could be touring in Europe next month, making plenty of money, and getting the appreciation he deserves.

He could be, but he won't be. He'll still be playing in dives for drunks who don't appreciate him, and taking home just enough money to get to the next gig. That's not romantic, or noble. That's living in a tiny box.

One thing I've learned, from studying Joe Vitale's *The Attractor Factor* and several other books is that we create our own world. We attract what we focus on.

We can have, do, or be anything we want. What we have, do, or are is the result of our inner landscape. It's actually one of the most profound discoveries I've ever encountered.

And it leads to a word of caution. Think about it. You attract what you focus on. If you carelessly focus on failure, scarcity, poverty, and unhappiness, then that's what you'll attract.

What do you see when you watch TV? What do you hear when you listen to the radio? What is the story in the books you read? What are the topics of the conversations you have?

That's what goes into your mind, and that's what you're focusing on. That's what you're going to attract.

The magic happens when you realize that you're responsible for your own outcome, and start doing what it takes to achieve the outcome you want.

When you start focusing on what you want to attract, you'll attract what you want.

When you write down your goals, and look at them every day, and take the action necessary to achieve them, you will achieve them.

Since you're creating your world, and since you have to live in it, doesn't it make sense to create a world of prosperity, success, and happiness?

Can you allow yourself a box that big?

"I'd Rather Fail Big Than Live Small"

I just got back from driving through the hill country and listening to Dan Kennedy interview Gene Landrum. As a gold member of Dan Kennedy's mentoring service, I get CDs every few weeks of Dan, or his partner Bill Glazer, interviewing a megasuccessful entrepreneur.

Lundrum gave Dan a delightful interview full of amazing stories taken from his books. And he made me feel like I belonged to a group, which is a feeling I don't get much—even when I'm hanging out with other musicians. You'd be amazed at how many artists and musicians are just sitting around waiting to be discovered while they continue to do the same thing all the other musicians and artists are doing.

Losers, losing by following losers. Not much of a plan, but it's pretty popular.

Until I discovered the Internet marketing world, I felt like the only square peg in a world of round holes. Listening to Dan's interviews makes me realize that I'm actually in good company. I'm a member of a group of entrepreneurs who follow Sam Walton's Rule #1.

Do you know Sam's "Rule #1?" He used it to build the most successful retail business in history. Do you want to know the secret that he used to make Wal-Mart unstoppable?

Keep reading.

His Rule #1 has been my credo all my life, and I've caught a great deal of shit for it; it turns out that Ayn Rand, Thomas Edison, Frank Lloyd

Wright, Henry Ford, H. Ross Perot, Donald Trump, Richard Branson, and most of my other heroes had the same credo.

Want to hear a story? Due to a bizarre and surreal series of circumstances, I found myself living the life of a high school dropout street hippie in 1973. I'd tell you the story, but you wouldn't believe me.

Franz Kafka's an amateur compared to East Texas wingnuts. I got on the wrong side of a town full of East Texas wingnuts and had to quit high school at seventeen.

My best option at the time was to move in with a house full of hippie musicians in the Montrose area of Houston. It was shelter, and we usually could scrounge food. Anderson Fair, a spaghetti restaurant that featured folk music, would feed us in return for a few hours of music, but only the zucchini spaghetti. You can live on zucchini spaghetti if you have to.

We played strip clubs and gay bars. We played for peanuts—literally.

After a year or so of this, on a hot and humid night, I accidentally drank a quart of mysterious tea, which caused me to take a psychic time-out. When I came back from visiting the red queen, I realized I needed to go to college.

So I walked in the early morning hours through the darkest, most dangerous part of Houston, to the bus station and took the bus home. I walked into the house as my father was drinking his morning coffee and announced that I was ready to go to college.

Skeptical, he suggested I get a job. After a year or so of manual labor, I finally made my way to North Texas State University (NTSU), on the strength of a good SAT score and a better audition with the piano faculty.

After a year of cutting down trees, I was probably the buffest piano major on the campus. While I was there, I designed and—with the help of a physics major buddy of mine—created the first laser light show in the Southwest. We had a running engagement at the Fort Worth Museum of Science and History.

After three years at NTSU, I sent an audition tape to the University of Texas and got accepted in their graduate composition program.

I still hadn't gotten my high school diploma. Technically, I was a high school dropout going to grad school.

I loved college. I ended up with music and English minors, but that only tells part of the story. I was a photography major, studying under

Gary Winnogrand. I studied journalism. I took art classes. I was in heaven. My degree plan was to not worry about getting a degree. I was getting an education.

After a few years, I got a glimpse of the naked underbelly of the modern classical music world and didn't like what I saw. A showdown with a famous composer during a seminar was the final straw.

He accused me of prostituting my art by making money writing commercials. What a crock! This was the same guy who financed his studio by doing sound effects for shampoo commercials. And some of the other ways he prostituted didn't have anything to do with his art.

I bailed on college and joined a rock band. Wouldn't you?

A short time later, we were touring with Cheap Trick, Heart, ZZ Top, The Climax Blues Band—it was a wonderful, exhausting, amazing experience.

At this point in my life, I was probably the best educated high school dropout rock star on the planet.

What's this got to do with Internet marketing, writing e-books, and running an international online business?

Everything!!

I think the most valuable benefit of my internet marketing lifestyle is the people I get to hang out with. After years of being a loner, I've got a peer group!

I get to hang out with Joe Vitale, who broke all the rules in the book publishing business, and went to number one twice on the national best seller charts—while the authors who played by the rules sat around and complained.

I get to hang out with Cindy Cashman, who made a million bucks by "writing" and promoting a blank book with a great title.

I get to hang out with Craig Perrine, who has achieved amazing success by breaking the rules in the internet list-building business.

And there are many others; the Internet marketing is a world populated with wild, intelligent, brave, and interesting people. These are the mavericks—the square pegs. I'm honored to know them.

All my life, I've heard "Get a *real* job!" The miserable, gray people— the ones trapped in the job they hate (which, according to Dan Kennedy's research, is 2/3 of the population)—wanted me to join them in their misery.

Parents. Teachers. Unsuccessful musicians. Bosses. Musicians have lots of bosses, because we keep a day job just long enough to book gigs, then we move on.

Television. Trump and Branson have TV shows, and that's a good start—but they're about hiring employees! The winners get a *job*!

You can bet your momma's egg money that Donald Trump doesn't want a job. Richard Branson doesn't want a job. They didn't get where they are by working for someone else. I think they should award prize money to the contestant who tells Donald Trump to take a flying leap at the moon, and starts his own business.

The education factories. Imagine what would happen if schools taught entrepreneurship instead of wage slavery? Our whole education system sucks lemons because it's based on a nineteenth century model, and designed to turn out workers—for jobs that haven't been available in decades! Factories that turn out waves of miserable, gray people—suffering through the week and living for the weekend.

What would happen if they taught people how to think, instead?

Family. Here's the big one. Anytime my family gets together, I get to hear about how I'm the one who's always "coloring outside the lines" from one of my relatives—he thinks he's insulting me!

That's the thing I'm proudest of and the key to my success. Nobody ever accomplished anything important, or grand, or *outrageous* by coloring inside the lines.

Following the rules is for losers.

Did you notice the list of heroes I put at the beginning of this chapter? They have a lot of things in common:

- They didn't wait for permission to be great. They just went ahead and did it.
- They didn't worry about credentials or diplomas. Richard Branson has an eighth grade education. Frank Lloyd Wright had about three months of formal schooling. All educated successful people, regardless of how much schooling they have, are self-educated. You can't trust the educators to educate you.
- They were *outrageous*! Branson and his hot-air balloons, and now space flights. Thomas Edison announcing the light bulb long before

he actually had created one. Everybody on that list listened to sage advice from the gray people and called bullshit on it. Then they went on to create a better world.

- They made their own rules. And then broke them.
- They had grand failures, followed by grand successes.

I tell my coaching clients, and I'll tell you—there ain't no such thing as failure. It's all data. To succeed *big* you may have to fail big. It's just a stretch of highway; you may have to go through some bad road to get where you're going.

The odds that we will be as successful as Thomas Edison or Richard Branson are small, even if we try. If we don't try, there's no chance at all.

I'd rather fail big than live small, wouldn't you? Especially knowing that "failing big" is just a stop on the way to "living large."

And what was Sam's Rule #1?

Here it is: Break the rules.

FAILING UP

I recently succeeded at failing at something new. That's always good. Mainly to record the Unseminars, I bought a couple of really nice 3-chip video cameras. Unlike my little handy cam, they have lots of options. Buttons, dials, switches, gauges. . . .

Until now, I've hired professional camera operators. Lately, I've wanted to just crank out some video products, and I wanted to do them with the big cameras. The problem was that I didn't have a clue how to use them.

So this weekend, I videotaped Joe Vitale's Beyond Manifestation 2 gathering. On day one, I failed miserably.

One of the quotes I live by is "If you're not failing on a regular basis, you're not trying near hard enough."

And failure? It's just data.

In case you're curious, the "A" setting on those big cameras stands for "aperture." As in "Aperture Preferred." Just like on an SLR camera.

I knew that. However, in the heat of the moment, I decided that "A" stood for "automatic."

Consequently, the video from the first day is a little—how to put it gently—I guess "unprofessional" would cover it.

However, over the course of the weekend, with a lot of help from some more knowledgeable people (thanks, Andy), I solved that and several other problems. By Sunday, the video was as good as possible under those lighting conditions. I don't know what Joe will end up doing with that video.

However, right now, while I'm writing, I'm transferring the video that Craig and I shot today onto the Mac. It's stunning. These Canon XL1s, when they're set correctly, create video that looks like film. Deep rich colors.

If I hadn't failed at my first try, or if I had given up when I failed, I wouldn't have this video. It will change a lot of lives; we really went deep on "the inner game." You can see what I mean at www.innergametv.com.

Tomorrow, we're going to do it again.

So, my recommendation is to find something you want to do and go fail at it. Give yourself permission to completely screw it up and go do it. With permission to fail, there's nothing you can't do—eventually.

WHERE GIANTS SLEPT

Today, me and my Portable Empire set up shop in historic Marfa, Texas. Oddly, I found myself thinking of Dan Kennedy, and his shadow, Bill Glazer.

When it comes to politics, Dan is an idiot. When it comes to marketing, Dan and Bill are geniuses. I think I've got every book Dan's ever written, and I recommend them highly. I'm in his "gold" mentoring program. When he starts talking politics, however . . .

What's Marfa got to do with marketing or Dan Kennedy?? I'm glad you asked.

Dan and Bill have a riff they do about Wal-Marts. Some stores just curl up and die when Wal-Mart hits town. Some stores just thrive. What makes the difference?

The stores that have a defined identity, and give the customer something they can't get at Wal-Mart, are the ones that thrive.

If you're a commodity, you're gonna die.

To thrive in a competitive environment, you've got to have a personality and a presence. You've got to have a well-defined product, and be the only source for that product.

If all you've got to offer is the same ole stuff that everybody else is offering, with the same tired cut-and-paste sales letters, then you're going to get lost in the crowd.

Here in far West Texas, some towns are just dying. Marfa, on the other hand, is thriving. Let me tell you just how much it's thriving.

You can pick up a rundown old adobe house here, if you're quick, for about $200,000. Movie stars, rock stars, and best-selling authors are lining up for the chance.

A few miles down the road, in Alpine, you can get a new house for half that. And Alpine is a pretty cool town, with a college and a very good blues bar.

Further down the road in Fort Stockton, they're basically giving land and houses away. Fort Stockton's a dump. It's got a Wal-Mart.

What's Marfa got that Fort Stockton doesn't have?

- A world-class bookstore that sells fresh-ground coffee. Free refills. Free Internet access. Wireless.
- Dozens of amazing art galleries.
- The Paisano Hotel, where the cast of the movie *Giant* stayed. You can rent the room where Elizabeth Taylor slept. You can get James Dean's room.
- A permanent Andy Warhol exhibit.
- The Chinati foundation, with acres of world-class art housed in old army barracks.
- The highest golf course in Texas.
- A rapidly increasing population of very interesting people.

And each time an interesting person moves there, and does something interesting, it just adds energy and attracts more interesting people. And the price of real estate goes up.

Marfa has a personality and a mix of benefits that you just can't get anywhere else.

Now, think about the successful Internet marketers you know. Can you see a correlation? The ones who are successful have worked hard to establish a personality and a brand.

- You know who Joe Vitale is, for example. If you read his blog, you know he's got a new car named Francine. You know he loves Hawaii. You know he writes a best-selling book about once a week. Joe's an easy example. Think of others.
- Dan Kennedy and his "no bull" books, with the picture of him on a huge bull.
- Jim Edwards and Mike Stewart and their Hee-Haw act.
- Gary Halbert and his "sh*t-weasel" stuff.
- Craig Perrine, the Maverick marketer.
- Armand Morin, and his twin Michael Lee Austin.

You can probably think of more. In fact, every successful marketer I know has spent time building his brand—his image—his story.

I initially resisted talking about my music career in my Internet marketing writing. Joe was adamant that I should. He was right. As far as I know, I'm the only Internet marketer who has a record deal and tours Europe. I'm the barefoot guy with a national steel guitar, in jeans and a T-shirt in a world full of suits. It's who I am.

The best advice I got when I started out was to "write in my own voice." Joe again. I was tempted to try and sound like the other marketers. I can do "marketingspeak," although I think it's silly.

There's an old saying, "If you're not the lead dog, the scenery never changes."

If you're carving your own path, you're the lead dog. The scenery is wonderful. In fact, the scenery is whatever you make it.

If you're trying to be somebody else—if you're not writing in your own voice and staying true to your own vision—well, your scenery is the south end of the guy in front of you.

Of course, you need to work on your inner game and your outer game. You need to tap into the power of the law of attraction (watch *The Secret*; watch it again).

You need to know how to make products, build your list, automate your business, and communicate with your customers.

But the most important thing you need to do, if you want to be successful, is also the easiest thing to do. You have to be you.

What's *your* story?

There's a lot of noise on the Internet right now about the "professional-izaton" of the Internet. There's a fear that as larger companies start moving their marketing online, Internet marketers are going to have to compete with them. Sounds like Wal-Mart is coming to town.

The solution that's being offered—and the people offering it have made millions of dollars by selling this fear and then selling their solution—is that Internet marketers need to be more like big corporations.

I submit that this is bull-poop. You can't compete with Time-Warner or Clear Channel Communications by becoming a cheap imitation of them. You can't afford to compete with them. And why would you?

That would be like the local clothing store putting up a tacky blue sign and hiring retirees to greet people at the door when they hear that Wal-Mart is moving in.

The little secret that Joe, and Dan, and all the other successful marketers know is that if you're saying something interesting, in your own voice, a certain percentage of the population is going to want to hear it from you.

Not everybody can take Gary Halbert's confrontational approach. I suspect that's fine with Gary, because the ones who like his voice want to hear and read (and buy) everything he says.

The same thing goes for the others I just mentioned, and the ones you're thinking of right now. It doesn't matter what the big corporations do, we're going to want to know what Joe Vitale, or Dan Kennedy, or John Carlton (I'm listing my favorites) have to say.

I was across the street from the bookstore in Marfa, taking pictures, when a movie star drove up in her new Jeep. She opened the door and draped one long leg over the side. I could almost hear a smoky tenor saxophone in the distance. The sun sparkled off her rich-girl hair.

From across the street, the saxophone faded into the distance, and I could hear a George Jones song playing on the radio. She waited until it was over before she turned off the Jeep and went inside. She could live in L.A. She may have a penthouse in New York. But because Marfa is so very Marfa, she's in Marfa. And so is her money.

THE MAGIC
OF UN-FRAMING

It's a Japanese woodblock kind of day in the Texas Hill Country.
Rain softens the already diffuse light that manages to get through the
clouds, muting the colors and softening the outlines of the hills and trees.
A good day to be indoors, working on a Portable Empire, looking out the
window.

What is "un-framing?" Well, it's like the old saying, "If the only tool you
have is a hammer, every problem looks like a nail."

What's a frame? That's the point of view, or the set of filters, through
which you see the world.

Here's an example. Let's imagine an old-growth redwood tree. Now,
look at it from the point of view of an ecologist. That tree provides shelter
for birds and other animals. It's a piece of history that has watched America change for hundreds of years. It's a piece of natural art. It's very valuable right where it is, and you wouldn't cut it down at gunpoint.

Now, look at it from the point of view of a carpenter. There are many
fine pieces of valuable furniture locked in that tree. You could build shelter with it. It's worth a fortune to you if you can cut it down.

It's the same tree. However, by changing the frame, it looks very different.

There's a great book called *The Power of Impossible Thinking* that ad-
dresses this. Highly recommended.

I used to frame the world from the point of view of a blues guitar
player. So, whenever I had a problem, I'd try to solve it from that point of
view.

There are lots of problems I couldn't solve, because I was using the wrong frame.

Take money problems, for example. Lots of people have them, and I did, too.

If your only solution to a money problem is to grab your guitar and go play in clubs, you're not going to solve your money problems. First of all, you're trading time for money, which is pretty ineffective. Second, there just aren't enough nights in the week, at a guitar player's salary, to fund much of a life.

So I (with a lot of help from Joe Vitale and a few others) decided to un-frame. Try it.

Here's what I did. I took a detailed inventory of my skills, talents, and assets.

Then I looked at my available market and asked, "How can I combine what I've got and what I can do to create something that the market will buy?" That's actually a magic question.

In my case, I had some musical equipment and some recording gear. I did some quick research into subliminal affirmations and binaural beats, and the Milagro Research Institute was born.

In the month of December 2005, we sold—well, it was about twice my annual income in my best year playing guitar. You can check some of those audios out at www.InstantChange.com.

Then, I discovered that I could take my recording gear on the road and record interviews—which is how www.EbookProblemSolver.com came about.

Well, the possibilities were just endless! I wrote a course on influence and persuasion and put it online at www.influence101.com.

If I had kept my old frame, none of those products would have been created—and I would probably be homeless.

About now, you should be asking yourself some questions.

"What frame am I using to look at the world?"

"What would the world look like without that frame?"

"How can I combine what I've got and what I can do to create something that the market will buy?"

Un-Framing
for Fun and Profit

L et's talk about un-framing. It's powerful stuff. Un-framing is a powerful exercise. I developed it to help me focus on new possibilities. At the time I came up with it, I was faced with some powerful decisions.

Basically, everything I was doing was *not* working. If something's not working, you do something else, right?

What? That's the hard part, isn't it?

At that time, I was framing the world through the filters associated with "blues guitar player." My answer to just about everything was "go play guitar." The problem with that frame is that playing guitar wasn't paying the bills. Heck, they repossessed my single-wide trailer house. That's the blues, all right, but it's not the answer.

So, I demolished my frame. That left everything else. Literally.

As humans, we can't see "everything else." We've got filters that keep us from being totally overwhelmed with the massive data storm that we live in. We've got social filters, political filters, relationship filters, and so on and so on. We've also got hard-wired filters that allow us to focus on, for example, driving a car or listening to a conversation in a crowded room.

It's impossible to see the world without filters, but it's fun and instructive to try. Try it. Visualize a universe with no boundaries and no limits. You can do anything. You can have anything. You can go anywhere. You're no longer who you were. You can be anything or anyone you want.

Like I said, it's impossible to see "everything else," but by trying, you can see some real interesting stuff.

A lot has changed in the last three years. My Internet marketing business is severely rocking. The success of the Unseminar1 videos was so freaking amazing that we're branching out into more, and much more ambitious video projects, starting with the Unseminar2 videos. I signed two book deals in 2006.

I can't say I planned any of this. If I had planned, I would have planned something much less ambitious, because I would have started from where I was, and used my past performance as a reference.

By unframing, I allowed the universe to drive. I'm at a much more interesting place than I would have been in if I was driving. Like Willie Nelson says, "Fortunately, we're not in charge."

It's time to unframe again. You may want to play along. If you're not exactly who you want to be, where you want to be, doing exactly what you want to do, this may be what you're looking for.

The filters I wanted to deconstruct were the ones that defined who I was and what I could do. I'd been remarkably successful at failing as a musician. The question was, What would I be successful at? And what is success, anyway?

Well, being homeless wasn't success. It must be something else.

It was remarkably useful to force myself to stop defining myself as a musician. That left "everything else." Cool.

The next step is to take an honest inventory of your skills, assets, passions, and talents. Back in 2004 those included, for me, a lot of guitars and keyboards, the ability to write and record music, an Internet connection and computer, the ability to write, and a couple of friends who were already into Internet marketing.

It's important at this step to have a firm determination to *not* do what you've done before. What else can you build with your assets?

In my case, a chance introduction to binaural beat technology opened the first door. I could use my music writing and recording assets to create what became the Milagro Research Institute audio programs. Today there are about 50 of them.

After I'd learned a little about marketing them (thanks, Joe!) and had started building my list, I got interested in writing e-books. Like our digital audios, e-books don't have any production cost, delivery cost, or storage cost. I discovered Clickbank and climbed that learning curve. Luckily, I had friends I could ask when I got confused (thanks, Bill!)

Being a newbie myself, I knew what problems newbies were having, so I wrote about those problems and the solutions I'd found. Those early e-books led to two publishing deals, but at the time, I was just trying to create a business. I was clueless, but I was just a little bit less clueless than the people who started after I did, so I wrote to those people.

You can see how far removed this is from loading up my guitar and amp and hopping on an airplane to go play blues, right? If I had stayed with what I was doing, I'd have no business, no book deals, no new luxury car, no new furniture, and so on.

Of course it was scary. It will be scary for you, too. After a while you'll learn that your comfort zone is the scariest place to be. Nothing happens there. The real action comes when you do the stuff you're scared of.

In my case, the next thing I was scared of was public speaking, so of course, I launched the Your Portable Empire Unseminar series. At the first one I was petrified. Nervous. Grumpy. Until it was over, and I realized that I'd pulled it off.

The Unseminar2 was much easier, although I still worked way too hard. We hung out, we played music, we had long, soulful conversations until five in the morning, and we put on a very successful, very powerful seminar. The attendees loved it!

How is your un-framing going? Are you able to remove your old frame and look at *all* the possibilities? What would you do if you knew you couldn't fail? That's a good place to start. Soon, you'll realize that there's no such thing as failure. It's all data.

If, and this is the big *if*, you realize that if something isn't working, it isn't working, and you stop doing it. That's the trick. If you want something else to happen, you have to do something else. Sometimes, you have to be a little bit brutal about it. For example, I kinda liked playing guitar on stage. I was comfortable there. I kinda miss it. The fact that, for me, a career in music is as dangerous as a coke habit is something I have to remember constantly.

As a matter of fact, right now it's a particularly seductive distraction. I just found out that one of my CDs has really taken off in Europe. I've moved into that rare territory where the label owes *me* money. I'm charting on some Internet-based music charts (and here's the Spinal Tap twist) including some in Japan. I could book a tour and try to capitalize on this odd, surprising success.

I'd lose my ass.

And yes, it's seductive. Like a crisp, unopened bottle of single-malt scotch would be seductive to a homeless alcoholic.

I think I'll pass for now and either find some new exciting ways to fail, or succeed. Been there, done that.

That brings us back to un-framing. Two and a half years later, my list of assets, skills, passions, and talents is different than it was.

- In my office, there is a world-class video editing suite, hooked into a state-of-the-art music recording studio. Two very professional video cameras. The rack of keyboards is wired into the production computer. The guitars (I think there are 12 of them, now—I lose track—blame it on red wine and eBay) are in their cases.
- My first book, *The Absolute Beginner's Guide to Internet Wealth*, is in production, and you're holding my second book. Last year, I didn't have any clue I was going to be an author!
- My assistant has scanned in about 20 very cool public domain books and is putting them online for a future marketing campaign.
- Unseminar3 is on the horizon.
- I've got some startling ideas for new Milagro audios.
- I want to take a ride in Joe's new car, and see if that inspires me to get a racecar of my own—although the Volvo is barely broken in.

Anything is possible. In an infinite universe, such as the one we live in, it just doesn't make sense to acknowledge *any* limitations.

The list goes on. I know things I didn't know back then. There are opportunities now that I didn't have before. See where un-framing can lead?

So it's with a combination of fear and excitement that I look at my lists. There are lots of opportunities to stretch out of my comfort zone.

I'm optimistically curious about what I'll do next. I think I'll find the opportunity that scares me the most. How about you?

Once you stop defining yourself as what you've done and who you were, and open up to the infinite possibilities available to you, what do you see?

What's Next?

One of the loops that runs through my mind regularly is "what's coming next?" What new, outlandish, outrageous experience, thing, or concept is going to come out of nowhere and change our lives?

Can you imagine a world without the Internet? Can you, really? It seems like it's always been there. I remember when Bill Hibbler first told me about Compuserve, which was a sorta precurser to the Internet. It seemed like magic. You could actually download a picture in less than an hour and see it right on your monitor. It even had some primitive forums and e-mail.

That was about a decade ago. Now, it seems like I've always had broadband high-speed Internet access.

And yet, for most of my life, if I wanted information I had to go to hard copy—newspapers (with a 24-hour lag) or magazines (months), or TV (spin, spin, spin). Now, we take for granted that we're entitled to immediate access to information.

As the migration of software from hard drive to online continues, our Empires can get even more Portable.

I've got shelves and shelves of books. They're kinda nice. Like vinyl records. Retro. Old-fashioned and inefficient.

I carry e-books around on my hard drive. It would be easy to upload them all to my server where I could access them from anywhere and share them.

Cell phones? Mine checks my e-mail, has room on it for lots of e-books, keeps my calendar up-to-date, and lets me actually make phone calls from pretty much anywhere. I've written chapters (short ones) for books on my cell phone. With a larger keyboard and the new, faster connection speeds, I could run my Portable Empire from a Treo 650.

What an amazing trip from the clunky bakelite "telephone" that we used to run to answer. I can remember heated discussions with my brother and sister when we were all teenagers. There was just one phone. For the whole family. And it was tied to the wall.

What got me thinking about "the next big thing?" An article in the *San Francisco Gate* newspaper.

Again, just imagine that. I'm sitting in Wimberley, Texas, reading a newspaper from San Francisco. Throughout the day, I'll scan a couple of British newspapers, one from Russia, scan the headlines in the *New York Times*, and check the local music listings in the *Austin Chronicle*—without leaving this chair.

Anyway, the article is about web2.0 sites, where the consumers are providing the content. Wikipedia is a web2.0 site; www.digg.com is another. They're great. They remind me of punk rock, back in the early days, or some of John Cage's projects. Anybody can be an artist, anybody can be a musician, and now, anybody can be a journalist or at least an editor.

You'd think that these sites would trend toward the lowest common denominator, but no. At digg.com, for example, you can zip down the rabbit hole to some techie magazine you've never heard of, click a link from there to a financial report that you'd never find on your own, and end up reading about how to build a wind-powered generator from recycled components.

It's the mastermind concept taken to plateaus that Napoleon Hill didn't even dream of. I love it.

FOR THE DREAMERS

H ave you heard of the movie *Factotum*, based on a Charles Bukowski story and starring Matt Dillon?

I was just reading the review in the *New York Times* and came across this great Bukowski quote:

> How in the hell could a man enjoy being awakened at 6:30 a.m. by an alarm clock, leap out of bed, dress, force-feed—there is, naturally, a scatological dimension to this—brush teeth and hair, and fight traffic to get to a place where essentially you made lots of money for somebody else and were asked to be grateful for the opportunity to do so?

What a great question! That question is at the heart of the Portable Empire concept. If there's a rational answer to it, I've never heard it. And yet, isn't that what most people do?

What are the options?

For the last week, I've been playing with a magazine that is just full of ads for business ideas. It's one of those with ads like "Make $2,000 a day from your home stuffing envelopes," or "How you can make $50,000 a year selling sno-cones," or "Join our pyramid scheme and get your family in your down-line and you can be a millionaire in six weeks."

Pages and pages of ads like that. Apparently, there's a market for it.

It's sad, really. But it points to the fact that we're all looking for something better. Something more. More freedom, more time, more toys. That and the fact that there are a lot of dreamers out there.

Recently at our mastermind meeting, we talked about our plans for the future. Our dreams.

It's rewarding to watch Joe grow. You would think that at his level, all the problems are solved. Wrong. They do get more interesting, and it seems to be about choosing the best of several lovely options. But when we started the group over two years ago, I couldn't imagine where Joe could grow to from where he was. He seemed to have it all. Now, he's miles further down the road, and what he's into now is some serious stuff. He's gone from making money to changing the world. I'm honored to be a part of it.

Bill's on a road trip. Cindy Cashman who, along with her sweetie, Mitch, is going to be the first couple married in space, is on vacation.

We all have our Portable Empires up and running, and we're long past the "selling sno-cones" phase in our career. Several of us have reached the point where we could stop working today, and meet our financial obligations for years comfortably. Possibly forever, in a couple of cases. Others of us are still building our Empires.

But the topic today was finding the balance between making money and doing what you love. My position is that there really isn't a choice there. If you're doing what you love, and doing it smart, you'll naturally make more money than you will if you're doing something you're lukewarm about. There's absolutely no future in doing something you don't want to do.

There are other philosophies. One of my buddies views his Portable Empire as a vehicle to take him to the place where he doesn't have to do anything. Season tickets at the ballpark, books from Amazon.com, and an open road for the sports car seems to be the plan.

That's cool, too. I remember one summer when I decided to read Will Durant's *History of Western Civilization*. That's all I did that summer, aside from basic dad duty. Downtime is good.

That was back in the not-so-good ol' days, when I was just getting my music career started. It's no wonder it didn't take off. I played just enough gigs to keep us in beans and tortillas, and we were living far below the poverty line. I could write an interesting e-book about how to live on almost no money. Probably should.

Today, I could easily take a year off and read, and maintain our current quality of life. However, I'm having way too much fun to stop now. In addition to my ongoing projects—e-books, audios, videos—I've discovered that I really like to teach the Portable Empire concept. There's a magic moment when you see it in somebody's eyes—they get it! There's always a little hesitation . . . "Can it be that easy?" "Yes."

Back at the mastermind meeting, when it came around to my turn, I had a question for the group: "Up to this point, I've been teaching people how to use their creativity to create e-books and other products, and market them. What do ya'll think about chunking up a level? Do you think it's possible to teach creativity, and the creative process?"

That's really my secret trick, ya know. I bring the same creative energy that I use to write songs or e-books to all facets of my marketing business. There's a creative aspect to configuring an autoresponder series. There's a creative aspect to almost anything—if you look for it, and know how to find it—and I think it's the trick to sending your business into hyperdrive.

I like to look at what everybody else is doing, and then explore doing the exact opposite. It's amazing how often that works.

It's a little like playing musical instruments. A good musician plays music. A generic musician plays an instrument. Once you learn how to play music, you can make music on just about anything. There are only 12 notes. Once you find them on an instrument, and figure out how to put the right notes together into triads, chords, and melodies, you're there.

I've used this little trick to learn piano, guitar, mandolin, bass—it's just a matter of chunking up and looking at it from "macro."

I think in our niche, the same principle might apply. You might frame yourself as an e-book author. But the same skills, plus a microphone, will make you an audio product creator. Add a video camera, and you're a video producer.

Chunk down, and it's a universe of distinct skills. Chunk up, and it's all the same thing.

It's that bigger chunk that interests me. I'm not sure where I'm going with this, or if that bigger chunk can even be taught. Stay tuned.

THE FUN ZONE

Some of my mentoring clients have been working on an issue that, while it's not exactly Internet marketing related, is an issue that most Internet marketing professionals have to deal with: courage.

Let's face it. It takes courage to do anything of value. Stretching yourself is scary stuff.

Unfortunately, the only way to handle scary situations without facing them is to avoid them. You can always hide in your comfort zone. Keep doing the things you're doing now. Of course, you'll keep getting the results that you're getting now.

To make something different happen, you have to do something different—and that means busting out of your comfort zone into the *Fun Zone*.

I wish I could say that I've conquered my own fears. It wouldn't be true. I can say that the things I fear now are much more interesting than the things I used to fear.

For example, I don't remember the last time I got stage fright. I do remember being twenty-three years old, hiding in the bathroom backstage, while several thousand people waited impatiently for my band to open for Cheap Trick in San Antonio. My stomach hurt. I was hyperventilating. I was a small town kid just a year out of college, and way out of my comfort zone.

Eventually we went on. The show went fine.

A couple of years ago, I headlined a similar size show in Germany. The sea of people stretched as far into the distance as I could see. I had a blast. The show rocked. My comfort zone had expanded quite a bit.

When I launched my first infoproducts, I had to deal with something very similar to stage fright. I had a lot of questions: "Who am I to think I have anything of value to say?" "Who would possibly buy an e-book from me?" "What if my e-book sucks?"

What was I worried about? Were the "e-book police" going to come barging into my home in the dead of night and take me away to "e-book prison" if I wrote a lousy e-book?

No.

It turns out that people liked my stuff, bought a bunch of it, and I've gone on to create a Portable Empire based on infoproducts. I've also got a side business teaching other people how to do it.

I've learned that everybody has their own voice, and that some people like mine. Some people will like yours, too.

Of course, I've failed. It happens. The dumb idea that sounded smart at the time ended up being just a dumb idea. A few times, I've failed pretty gloriously.

About a year after the Cheap Trick tour, we were headlining the Armadillo World Headquarters in Austin. The show was sold out. A couple of guys from ZZ Top were backstage, and they had brought along a few models that had been featured in *Penthouse* magazine that month. Eric Johnson was tuning up his Strat—he was going to play our encore with us. Our manager brought a case of Dom Perignon, which we were drinking straight from the bottle.

My father and girlfriend were in the audience. I wanted them as far from backstage as possible.

At that time, I was a keyboard player, and I had a brand new Moog Polymoog keyboard. It was expensive. It was a technological marvel. The only thing wrong with it was that occasionally it didn't work. It was a total crapshoot from night to night, and the only reason I used it at all was because there wasn't anything better available. And when it did work, it was glorious.

About two-thirds of the way through the show it was time for my solo. The rest of the band left the stage. The lights went down, except for the spotlight on me. I hit the button on the synthesizer that would start the sequencer. And nothing happened. Ulp.

Instead of a glistening stream of electronic sounds that would mesmerize the audience, there was a long, extended, fartlike blatt. Great.

I turned the synth off, which created a massive *click* through the Armadillo's huge PA system. Then I turned it back on.

Click. It took a few minutes to power up. I hit the button that would start the sequencer so I could do my solo. Nothing happened. Ulp, again.

I jumped up, knocking my stool into the crowd, ran backstage, and hid. Wouldn't you?

We eventually finished the show, and you know what? Nothing bad happened!

I was certain that the reviews would focus on my equipment malfunction. I thought it was possible that the "hip musician police" would haul me off and shoot me in some dark pocket of the forest. I was sure that the band would fire me the next day—if they waited that long. Nope.

The reviews focused on the music. Eventually, I got a keyboard that worked reliably. (Eventually, I switched to guitar and things got really interesting.) My music career lasted another 35 years and counting, and nobody has ever mentioned that particular failure to me since then. Big drama in my head. Out in the real world, it really wasn't that big a deal.

In May 2005 I promoted an Internet marketing seminar. The Unseminar1.

Boy, was that out of my comfort zone. However, I've decided that my comfort zone is the most dangerous place on the planet. Staying in my comfort zone kept me broke and miserable for decades. So I put on a seminar.

It was terrifying to ask the speakers to speak at my event, and I was absolutely dumbfounded when they all agreed. It was very scary for me to promote it. So I just sent e-mails to my list (they're an understanding bunch) to test the sales letter. And sold out the darn thing in six hours. Attendees signed up from Holland, Australia, New Zealand, Canada, and over a hundred more wanted to get in and couldn't.

I had a few freakouts. The power went out while we were setting up the cameras. There was some alien interference with the wireless microphones.

By the time Joe showed up Saturday for his breakout session, I was a mess. Sleep deprived, nervous, and absolutely sure that the unseminar was going to completely spin out of control, leaving me a fugitive from the "seminar police," who would come to my house in the dead of night and. . . .

Hey, wait a minute. That sounds familiar. Joe assured me that everybody he talked to was raving about how good the un-seminar was. All the speakers and attendees were enjoying themselves.

I pulled myself together and went about the business of running a seminar. At the end of the un-seminar, I got a standing ovation from the speakers and attendees. Since then, I've gotten e-mails from most of them thanking me for putting on the event.

As I edit the video, I'm amazed. I look confident. I'm full of b.s., laughing, and professional.

Who knew? Not me.

I had a lot of fun editing that video. Who am I to edit video? I learned to edit video the same way I learned to engineer and produce records. I got some gear and started doing it. Do you think the video police are gonna show up in the middle of the night if I screw up? Naw. They don't exist.

The reason I'm sharing all of this is to scare you out of being scared. I could have stayed safely in my comfort zone. I could have walked out of the first big concert I played, and gone back to waiting tables. I could have not launched my first infoproduct. I could have not put on the un-seminar, and I could have not videotaped it.

That's scary. Me, at fifty-one, waiting tables. But that's where I would be if I hadn't left my comfort zone for someplace much more comfortable.

Now, I'm trying to maintain a frivolous curiosity. I recommend it highly. Go do something you can't do. Just notice your fear in passing and do it anyway.

Then, go find something else you can't do—and do it. The real fun is just outside your comfort zone.

ALL THE SUCCESS
YOU CAN STAND

T. Harv Eker has it right. You have to change your inner "wealth thermostat" before you can accept, and keep, wealth at a greater level than you're used to.

Two and a half years ago, when I first discovered Internet marketing, I lived in a trailer house and drove a Ford truck with over 200,000 miles on it. And to be honest, I was living beyond my means. That's where my wealth thermostat was stuck.

A little less than a year ago, I bought a new car: a Scion XB. It was imminently practical, inexpensive, and, well, "cute." I called it the Mighty XB, and put 20,000+ miles on it. Then some jerks stole it, along with a bunch of other cars, while I was in Atlanta.

However, when I bought it, I could have afforded a lot more car. I could have been more comfortable. I could have been safer. My wealth thermostat just wasn't set high enough to allow me to have that car.

Eventually, I think I'm headed for a Maybach. I don't have any doubt that I'll have one. I remember standing on the MaximilianStrasse in Munich with a group of German friends as one drove by. My German friends are used to excellent automobiles (my drummer is a BMW dealer, and has several), but they froze. Just completely stopped moving and watched in awe as the Maybach rolled down the street.

Right now, I'd feel uncomfortable driving that car. I'm just not there yet. Wealth is all in your mind, and my mind hasn't grown enough to allow me to have that car.

My wealth thermostat is rising, though. A good indicator that it is rising: Less than a year after I got the XB, I'm able to allow myself a new Volvo V-70. It's about the safest car on the road, and like the cute librarian who dances on the weekends, she will flat move when you motivate her.

I listened skeptically when Joe, Craig, Bill, and, more recently, Alex Mandossian talked about the feeling of prosperity you get when you drive a nice car. To me it sounded like they were just justifying driving nice cars.

The joke's on me. They were right. As I sit back in the comfortable seat, looking at the world framed through the windshield of the V-70, totally supported by the very comfortable seats (with adjustable lumbar support, y'all!), the world does look different to me. And my mind works differently, too. I'm becoming the sort of person who would drive a nice car.

I used to have real problems with conspicuous consumption. Coming from a mindset of poverty, it just seemed wrong to drive big, nice cars while some people had to walk. I still get an echo of that occasionally, but I remind myself that it's an infinite universe. Everybody can have the wealth they want. There's no shortage of anything, once you do the mental work to attract that wealth, and the much harder mental work of allowing yourself to accept it.

All I do is create information products and market them. Then I do it again. Over time, I've developed multiple streams of passive income. This gives me a great deal of freedom, and I'm not just talking about the freedom to drive luxury cars. There's some interesting territory beyond the big house and fancy car.

I was talking to a friend I respect very highly about this. She's kind of my benchmark for how to live your life. I told her that I had a strategy to generate 1 million dollars a year, and that I was right on target toward putting that strategy in place. I was probably a little smug about it.

She said, "So what?"

That kind of knocked me back in my saddle a little. "What do you mean, SO WHAT? You knew me when my earned income was about ten grand a year. Now I'm talking, seriously, of being a millionaire. That's progress, right?"

She looked at me kinda funny, slanting her head to one side. Then she explained to me about Maslow's ladder, and how success looks like big cars and big houses when you're down on the bottom rungs. As you get closer to the top, you get a better view of what success really means. You come to realize that cars and houses are not going to satisfy you. There's something on the higher rungs that is much more interesting, and powerful, and valuable than just flashy assets.

Of course, I'd studied Maslow's hierarchy in school, but I've spent so much time on the bottom rung, where just keeping food on the table was taxing my abilities, that I hadn't spent any time wondering what the top of it looked like.

My friend lives on the top rungs, way past cars and houses. Of course, she's got a nice car and a nice house. She's climbed those rungs, too. I think this is fascinating.

As I look back on the last two years, I'm weak with gratitude for the changes in my life. But, the funny thing is, I'm the same guy who struggled all those years. I've got the same degrees from the same colleges. I'm not any smarter now than I was then. I'm working a lot less and enjoying my work a lot more.

So what changed? Well, developing the strategies I use in my business was important, but more important, I think, were the changes I made in my attitude and belief system that allow me to succeed.

I had the tools I needed all along.

It sounds like magic, doesn't it? It sure feels like magic. And it sure is fun.

The "funnest" part is that there are so many more options available now.

I'm not sure where I'm headed with all of this. I'm looking forward to some deeper conversations with my friend about the cloudy peaks at the top of Maslow's hierarchy.

THIN SLICING THROUGH THE INFORMATION OVERLOAD JUNGLE

I recently asked my list what problems they wanted help with, and the problem that ranked #1 is "How do I deal with information overload?"

One reader claimed to have downloaded over a million pages of free information during the holidays. Nobody is going to read a million pages of anything. Not in this lifetime.

I can give you some strategies that will help you cut through the fog and focus on what you need to focus on. Let's reframe the problem so we can get a handle on it.

We need to decide what's important and what isn't. Then we need to focus on what's important and let the unimportant stuff go. You have to be firm about this. Either something is relevant or it isn't. You know immediately. If it's not relevant, delete it.

That doesn't mean that reading for fun is a bad thing. I occasionally curl up with a glass of Shiraz and a Kinky Friedman or O. Henry book. From reading Kinky, it's obvious that he curls up with O. Henry, too. I love to watch Nero Wolfe solve mysteries. I've reread the *Hitchhiker's Guide to the Galaxy* and all the sequels, until I can recite pages of the stuff from memory, and I look forward to reading it again. Maybe it's the Shiraz, but I find something new and hilarious every time I reread Douglas Adams.

That's not what I'm talking about. I'm talking about the hundreds of e-mails, e-books, and offers that land in your mailbox every week. I'm talking about the conflicting information you get on important subjects like, for example, copywriting.

The solution is "thin slicing." I got that concept from a book called *Blink* by Malcolm Gladwell, who also wrote *The Tipping Point*. Both of these books are required reading, in my opinion.

Gladwell proves, using scientific data and fascinating stories, that we can rely on our intuition, in some cases, to make instant decisions that are more accurate than decisions made after minutes, hours, or months of thought.

You can gather enough data in two seconds, in some cases, to come to a firm and precise conclusion about very complex problems.

The data you need is in the thin slice of data that your subconscious needs to make that decision, and it gathers that data at light speed. All the other data is unnecessary and may lead you to a wrong conclusion. It can certainly confuse you, and confusion is an unproductive state to be in when you're trying to build a Portable Empire or do just about anything else productive.

One way to use thin slicing is to be very clear about what's important to you. Train yourself. Practice. Write down the things that are essential for you to know, and learn to recognize them instantly.

For example in my business, I've narrowed down what I do to three things.

1. I make products.
2. I sell them.
3. I attract subscribers to my list and get to know them, and let them get to know me.

In terms of my business, if the information falls under one of those categories, I'm interested. Maybe. Actually, I slice it thinner than that.

One of the things I need to learn to sell my products is copywriting. Maybe it's because I have lunch every week with a world-class copywriter, Joe Vitale, and two other guys who are darned good copywriters, Craig Perrine and Bill Hibbler—but I'm pretty convinced that writing copy is not one of my strong suits.

Joe writes sales copy that makes me swoon with admiration and envy. Seriously. Joe writes sales copy like Stevie Ray Vaughan played guitar. Like Yo-Yo Ma plays cello. Like Picasso painted. Joe's that good.

Craig and Bill aren't quite in Joe's league (at copywriting; they have other strengths), yet, but they can write circles around me with one hand tied behind their back. They're awesome.

I'm learning. I still have to write copy. Hiring a good copywriter costs thousands of dollars. Hiring a great copywriter to write one sales page can cost more than your parent's house. For my smaller promotions, I just have to write the copy or it doesn't get written. So I have to study copywriting. Here's where the thin slicing comes in.

Of all the copywriters who teach copywriting, I've chosen to study Joe. I went to his $5,000 weekend copywriting seminar, and the textbook he created for that course is right here on my desk. It's stained and dog-eared. I've got the videos of that seminar, and I watch them when I need inspiration.

I've also studied with Ted Nicholas, Brian Keith Voiles, John Carlton, and several others. I've heard them speak at seminars, and I've read their books. I read John Carlton's blog religiously.

Sometimes, Ted will say something that absolutely refutes something that John says. Ted writes like a courtly gentleman. John writes like a street fighter, or like the rock guitarist he used to be. He's sold a forest of golf clubs; he writes gutsy copy for guys.

Brian has a style of writing that is almost psychic. I don't think anybody but Brian can write like he writes. Joe says things that none of the other copywriters agree with.

So, when I'm studying copywriting I use Joe to establish the framework, and then thin slice the rest. If John says something that fits on Joe's framework, I pull it out and add it to my working data. If what he says conflicts with Joe, I ignore it. Immediately.

That doesn't mean that Joe is necessarily better at teaching copywriting than John. They're both brilliant. You just can't follow both of them. They contradict each other.

If my goal was to be the world's best copywriter, I might take a different position. That's not my goal. My goal is to sell products. I don't need to be great at copywriting; I just need to be good enough to make the sale.

Each of those gurus has dozens of strategies for coming up with great headlines. I don't need hundreds of strategies for coming up with headlines. I don't even need two. I need one that works for me.

You probably noticed that I define my scope in a pretty narrow way.

Because I create products, I'm not real interested in private label products that other people create. Occasionally, I'll promote a product for a friend or because I think it's a great fit for my list, but I'm not looking for them. I am militantly uninterested in the latest affiliate strategies.

So, if I get an e-mail about private-label products, or how to be a dynamite affiliate, or—the list of things I don't need to know is very large—Search Engine Optimization—RSS—whatever today's most popular distraction is, I delete it immediately.

Those things are important, but not to me. They're not what I do, and if I take the time to chase them all, I'm stealing time away from the things I know will make me money.

So, what's the solution to information overload? I just do three things.

1. Get clear on what it is that you do. If you're just starting out, here's the most important hint you'll ever get: All of the gurus are right. Pick one.

   That's right. One. Pick one and follow their advice. Buy their products. Read their newsletters. Use your intuition to find the one that resonates with you and then immerse yourself in their strategies, and make those strategies yours.

   I learned that at the first Internet marketing seminar I attended about two years ago.

   All of the speakers contradicted all of the other speakers. And they were all right. If you did exactly what any one of the speakers recommended, you would be successful. If you did what any two recommended, you'd get lost.

2. Decide where you want to go. If you want to go to New York, find the guru who can direct you to New York. If you listen to them, chances are you'll end up in New York.

   However, if you also listen to the guy giving directions to San Francisco while you're listening to the directions to New York, and then somebody else starts telling you how to get to Houston—you're not going anywhere. At least, not anywhere interesting or profitable. This takes practice.

3. Focus on the things that help you do what you do. Trust your intuition, and learn how to quickly recognize what's useful, and use it. Learn to recognize "noise" and delete it.

MAGICAL
MARKETING TOUR

This morning, I was taking my son Patrick to school. We were listening to the Beatles' "Sergeant Pepper's Lonely Hearts Club Band." Patrick's in the process of making demos in his bedroom recording studio, which provides me with steady proud daddy moments.

Anyway, we were talking about the Beatles. They had an interesting problem. Their drummer, compared to other drummers at their level, was—not to put too fine a point on it but compared to, say, Ginger Baker (Cream) or Charlie Watts (Rolling Stones)—"weak."

Ginger and Charlie had strong jazz backgrounds, and playing rock music was really "playing down" for them. Not the case with Ringo Starr.

They also had another problem, one that would have destroyed a lesser group. Their best lead guitar player was singing and playing bass. Their next best guitar player was also singing lead and providing the strong rhythm guitar that drove the band.

That left George Harrison, who, in time, became a wonderful guitar player. However, when he joined the band, he was the same age as my son, seventeen, and compared to the lead guitar players in other bands of the time—Peter Green, Eric Clapton, Jeff Beck, just to name a few—he was pretty weak, too.

I can just imagine John Lennon and Paul McCartney sharing a couple of pints at the pub, talking this over. They weren't about to let little things like this keep them from conquering the world. They were building an empire, and realized, rightly, that problems can be turned into opportunities.

They might have had a "what's working, what's not working" meeting. They knew they had great songs, great harmonies and melodies, a great producer, and an unlimited budget, which gave them access to symphony orchestras and talented session musicians.

By recognizing the weakness of their drummer, they came up with some of the most creative rhythm tracks in history.

There are tracks where Paul played drums. There are hand-claps, tambourines, anvils, animal sounds, backward cymbals, car horns, all used as drums. Much more interesting than just a "good" drummer, but if they'd had a good drummer, they would never have looked for the alternatives.

There are places on the album, *Abbey Road*, for example, where there are two complete drum kits playing at the same time, while a third snare is accenting the downbeat. By using technology and creativity, they were able to overcome what could have been a devastating problem.

They were equally creative with the guitar problem. On the early albums, they solved the problem by ignoring it, and the lead guitar parts were so simple that pre-teens in bedrooms all over America were able to learn them. Some of them bought the albums because the guitar parts were simple. I know, I'm one of them. With just a few notes, I could be a Beatle. Brilliant.

Later, they would outsource. There are oboe, trumpet, violin, kazoo and "na, na, nas" where a band with a great guitar player would have put guitar solos.

When they absolutely had to have a world-class guitar solo, they hired Eric Clapton to play it. Good choice. That beautiful solo on George's song, "While My Guitar Gently Weeps," is Eric, and it's one of the high points of western civilization, in my opinion.

On Abbey Road, again, toward the end of side 2 (yes, I'm that old), there is a three-guitar shoot-out, where George, Paul, and John take turns playing their hottest licks. John always said that he won the shootout, but if that's Paul on the Les Paul, I'd disagree.

Of course, by the time the "White" album came out, the Beatles weren't really speaking to each other, and this led to John, Paul, and George playing all the instruments on their songs or hiring "ringers," which is also how I make my CDs. Technology rocks. I'm assuming Ringo spent some time at the pub.

Now, all these years later, what lessons can we learn from the Fab Four?

- *Every problem is an opportunity.* We all have our gifts—our talents and abilities—but none of us has *all* of them.

  Be honest with yourself about what your gifts and talents are. In the places where you're weak, realize that you are free. It's liberating, once you get used to it. If you want an e-book empire but can't write—congratulations. You've got the public domain, and there have been some serious fortunes made with public domain works. You can go to www.elance.com and hire a writer; they're cheap. You can speak your thoughts, and record them, and sell the recordings. You can interview others and record the interview—products are everywhere.

- *Don't let the lack of some resource stop you from making your dreams come true.* Once you know what you don't have, you can creatively find ways to use what you do have to get your project done.

  Excuses are wonderful, aren't they? Once you've got a good one, you can hide behind it for years. Recognize excuses for what they are, delete them, and turn your problems into opportunities. If you don't have money, a huge list, or a clue, team up with someone who does, and succeed, anyway.

  Then write a book about how you did it, and sell the book.

Keep your eyes open. Opportunities are everywhere.

"Strawberry Fields . . . Nothing Is Real . . . Strawberry Fields Forever"

I've still got the 45rpm vinyl of that. If you're anywhere near my age, you probably owned one, too.

The label has that yellow and orange swirl that Capitol Records used.

Those swirly labels constituted the first early music videos. I used to put on stacks of 45s and sit, absolutely hypnotized, staring at the swirly labels spinning round and round and round.

And that was way before the "lost years." If I was high, it was from following the mosquito foggers around.

On the other side is "Penny Lane." The record label claims that both songs were written by "Lennon and McCartney," but that's legal fiction. "Penny Lane" is Sir Paul's melodic remembrance, and it lilts magically and hypnotically as it introduces you to the fabulous characters.

"Strawberry Fields," on the other hand, is all John Lennon. It's a dreamy, image-filled trip that doesn't make any sense at all if you read it with your conscious mind. I understood it immediately.

According to some amateur psychologists, you can tell a whole lot about a person if you can find out who their favorite Beatle was. Mine was John.

Now that they've released the Gulf of Tonkin documents, our worst fears have come true about the Vietnam "police action." Today's news is even more bizarre. Historians are going to have a hard time explaining this period of time, unless they understand hypnotism and persuasion psychology.

My more intelligent friends tell me to not read the newspaper. I look at it like I would look at a wreck on the side of the highway. It's awful. I can't help it.

So I've got my narrative about the Vietnam police action, and my narrative about the current unpleasantness. I suspect they're different from yours, and I believe them strongly because they're based on the truth as I perceive it, which according to Richard Bandler is a pile of bunk.

Have you read *Frogs into Princes* by Richard Bandler? I was a little late getting to it, but now I'm reading all the Bandler I can find. He studied with Milton Erickson, and has done a lot of work. If there is a jedi master walking the planet today, it's probably him.

Humans need to put their experiences in narrative form. We all have our story. Some people use their stories to create excuses. I used to be one of those people. It was my parents' fault. It was my teachers' fault. My failure was just about anybody's fault but mine.

Here's where the fun comes in. Once you start studying social psychology, and especially start getting into Bandler, John Grinder, and Erickson, you come up against some odd facts. And the fact that they're facts is what makes them odd.

For example: Everything you think of as your story—everything you think you remember—is wrong.

That's right.

You are absolutely making up your personal history.

Odd.

But true.

No two people see an event the same way. When you allow those perceptions to marinate for a few decades, the resulting stew has nothing at all to do with objective reality—whatever that is.

On the rare occasions that I hang out with my brother and/or sister, this becomes obvious. It's like we were raised in a different home, by completely different parents. Our memories do not have anything at all in common besides geography.

This gives us the opportunity for amazing freedom, if we want it. It could also give us the opportunity to hide in a cave, flipping our lips with our fingers and saying, "Buh, buh, buh . . ." It's mind-blowing.

Nothing is real. We can then choose our past, right? Right. There are therapists out there right now installing false memories and upgrading people's stories.

Well, if we can choose our past, we can also choose our future.

Joe Vitale writes in his book *The Attractor Factor* that we can all be happy right now by choosing to be happy. That works for me.

I think everybody sets arbitrary goals for their happiness. They tend to ratchet up in value and difficulty as they get more successful.

I can remember thinking as a teenager, "If I only had a car, I'd be happy." Of course, where it all falls down is the day you get the car and then take the internal inventory and realize that you're not really happy. You don't really want a car.

What you want is a gold Bentley with spinning wheels and canary yellow leather interior and black and red fuzzy dice hanging from the zircon-encrusted rearview mirror that plays movies from the DVD player hidden in the trunk.

Posh. Won't work. What you want is to be happy, unless you don't want to be happy, in which case you're probably not.

I'm not sure where all this is heading. Nothing is real, nothing we remember actually happened the way we remember it, and all we have to do to be happy is decide to be happy.

I see the freedom in it. The ability to view each intersection in our life as a choice point, reach into our incredible banquet of choices, and pull out the one that tastes the best and chomp on it.

At least that's how I'll remember it.

PORTABLE EMPIRE
HEADS WEST

The benefits of running a home business become even more obvious when you leave home. Especially if your home business is a Portable Empire.

One of the goals I've had is to increase my choices. We see these choice points go by: when someone cuts in front of you in traffic, when your mate says something cutting, when some business strategy just doesn't work—every moment of every day is a choice point.

The trick is to meet each choice point with the largest and most effective arsenal of choices. For example, let's take traffic. When someone cuts in front of you, what are your choices?

There was a time when my only choices were: (1) yell, lean on my horn, and give the one-finger salute or (2) tailgate the offender, and try to get them to pull over so we could "talk."

That's a fairly impoverished set of choices.

What are some other options? Well, every time someone cuts you off in traffic, you could mentally add a dollar to your personal pleasure fund. At the end of the week, you could make a rule that you have to spend the entire amount in your personal pleasure fund on something that you find relaxing. You'll start to look forward to rude drivers, and be grateful for them.

Or every time someone cuts you off in traffic, you could recite an ancient Haitian curse that you just made up on the spot that is guaranteed to make their noses and their reproductive organs exchange places. Imagine that . . .

The point is to realize that you are in control, and you can meet every choice point with a creative range of choices. You don't ever have to do the expected or obvious.

I think one of the secrets of my success is that I don't know what I'm doing, or what should be done. It gives me an alarmingly fresh outlook on Internet marketing. Because I don't know what I'm supposed to do at a choice point, my range of choices is much larger.

It drives my more traditional nerd marketer friends crazy, of course, but as I keep cranking out e-books and information products, and they keep selling, they've stopped threatening to banish me to the Bandera Home for the Bewildered. For now.

The trick about "work" is that it's the boat that carries you where you want to go. It's the means through which you achieve your goals. Only rarely is attachment to the boat a good idea. When you get to your destination, it's okay to get out of the boat.

Or not.

Some people like riding in the boat. That's cool. In an infinite universe, such as the one we happen to be living in, there is no shortage of resources. That's the big news.

The boat is fuelled by ideas. If you're using any other fuel, you're wasting your time. The better the fuel, the faster the boat goes. And the less time you have to spend in the boat to get where you want to go. If you've got great ideas and happen to like to work, you can end up going quite a long way.

Right now, most of my friends who have jobs are trading time for money. We know that doesn't work. That's a slow boat.

When you really get in the groove, though, is when you're not working—you're playing the game. It isn't work at all.

I love the Internet marketing game. It's not hard. You identify a need, you provide a solution, and you tell your list about it. Like chess, the moves are easy to learn. You can actually play a game using memorized moves.

You can be successful at internet marketing by just following the directions on the side of the box—that's what metawebs, adsense, and the other systems processes do. Follow the directions, and they make money.

To me, it's far more interesting to get into the game. I first noticed this when I was making records—yep, back in the days when you recorded on tape and the final product was pressed into a vinyl disc.

There are times when I was recording music and I would lose all track of time. I was totally hypnotized by the act of creation, and there is nothing like hitting the playback button and realizing that you have created a beautiful thing and it is good.

I can get the same rush from writing and creating products (what time is it, anyway?).

I said that work was a boat that takes you where you want to go. If you're very, very lucky, it becomes a magic carpet that you really enjoy riding. That's what the Portable Empire is all about. Realizing that life is an adventure and putting that sense of adventure into every single thing we do.

So where do you want to go?

KALI, THE BENEVOLENT DESTROYER

In Hindu mythology, Kali is the symbol for the cycle of destruction and creation. She is identified with the darker side of the feminine. It's important to remember that the destruction she represents is a necessary trough in the cycle of destruction/creation. You can't have one without the other.

The Tao Te Ching talks about this concept in gentler tones. It's the hole in the vase that allows you to carry water. It's the door in the wall that allows you to enter the room. The value of what is, is made available by what isn't.

This can be a tough concept, but I've found it very useful.

Sometimes, to attract something that works into your life, you have to get rid of what doesn't work. To have what you want, you may have to give up what you don't want.

But, bottom line, you have to make room in your life if you're going to attract something new.

For example, when I was first beginning my Internet marketing journey, a year and a half ago, I was spending up to five nights a week playing in bars. This involved loading my truck with my music gear, driving (sometimes hundreds of miles) to the gig, setting up the gear, playing music for four hours, and then the whole process repeated in reverse.

Sometimes the sun was rising over the Texas hills as I drove into my driveway, which is real romantic sounding unless you're the one actually dragging home at six in the morning. Of course, I was useless for the rest of the day, and I'd do it again the next night.

In Texas, you can count on making, on average, about 50 bucks for playing in a bar. Sometimes more. Often less.

Once I made the commitment to build my online empire, I had to stop doing that. It was a leap of faith. The money I made from playing guitar wasn't much, but it was all I had.

But I couldn't have both. I couldn't continue to wear myself out playing bars and still have the energy to create and market information products.

Kali swung her terrible sword, and I just stopped playing bars.

And a funny thing happened. Almost immediately, positive things—events, opportunities—rushed in to fill the vacuum.

Another funny thing happened. As part of my business creation, I put myself through a sort of master's class in learning to think like a successful marketer. I filled my mind with books and articles about success, positive thinking, creative visualization. I basically reprogrammed my mind.

I had a lot of help, for which I am very grateful. But it was the result of a massive commitment on my part to delete the limiting beliefs and "loser" mind-set, and replace them with beliefs and thoughts that would result in success.

Here's the funny part. As I became more aware of my "self-talk" and belief structure, I became less interested in hanging out with people who were stuck in loser mode. You know the ones. In Texas, there are actually guys with Born to Lose tattooed on their arms. A lot of the musicians I knew had it tattooed on their minds. Free booze and easy lovin' are part of the attraction, but there's also a "beautiful loser" syndrome endemic among musicians that encourages failure.

Finally, I had to delete most of them from my life. And the strangest thing happened. A whole new group of friends appeared to fill the vacuum. Wonderfully creative people whom I never would have met if I hadn't made room for them.

This brings to mind the story of the general who had his troops gather on the shore and watch as their ships burned. The general had ordered the ships burned so that his soldiers, stranded in a foreign land, would understand that they had to either win (and build new ships) or die. This was brutally motivating. They won.

On a side note, I have heard two highly successful businesspeople give a passionate lecture about deleting the word "try" from your vocabulary.

Think Yoda. There is no "try." If you're going to do something, do it with all of your heart, and with a full intention of accomplishing what you set out to do. It is a waste of your time, for example, to "Try" internet marketing. Don't bother.

It's a waste of your time to "try" to have a successful relationship, or learn to play the piano, or skydive. Either do, or don't do. In the spirit of Kali, both of those speakers were women, by the way.

So, what's this got to do with you? It depends. If your life looks exactly the way you want it to look, and you've got everything—spiritually, psychologically, financially—that you want, you can probably just nod sagely and go on.

If you're like most people, there is an opportunity here for you. Do a "what's working" inventory. Brutally (but compassionately) inventory your life, and make a list of what's not working and delete everything on it.

Just like that.

Visualize Kali with her sword, and get rid of what's not working.

You'll be amazed at how quickly the void is filled with things that do work.

If you're going to be an infoproduct marketer, and you can't seem to find the time, now is the time to look at the things standing between you and success, and make the decision to choose success. This means *not* choosing the things that are causing you to fail. Delete them. Stop doing them. Make room for success in your life, and leave no room for the distractions.

This works for whatever your goal is. If you're going to do it, don't "try"—DO.

BIBLIOGRAPHY

Bandler, Richard, and John Grinder. *The Structure of Magic.* Palo Alto, CA: Science and Behavior Books, 1975.

Bernays, Edward. *Propaganda.* Brooklyn, NY: Ig Publishing, 2004.

Byrne, Rhonda. *The Secret.* New York, NY: Atria Books, 2006.

Cameron, Julia. *The Artist's Way.* New York, NY: Penguin, Putman, Inc., 2002.

Cameron, Julia. *The Vein of Gold.* New York, NY: Penguin, Putman, Inc., 1997.

Cialdini, Robert. *Influence: The Psychology of Persuasion.* New York, NY: Harper Collins, 2006.

Eker, T. Harv. *Secrets of the Millionaire Mind.* New York, NY: HarperBusiness, 2005.

Gage, Randy. *Why You're Dumb, Sick, and Broke and How to Get Smart, Healthy and Rich.* Hoboken, NJ: John Wiley and Sons, 2006.

Gladwell, Malcolm. *The Tipping Point.* New York, NY: Little, Brown and Company, 2002.

Gladwell, Malcolm. *Blink.* New York, NY: Little, Brown and Company, 2007.

Hill, Napoleon. *Think and Grow Rich.* Meriden, Conn: Ralston Society (originally published 1938).

Moore, Christopher. *Lamb.* New York, NY: HarperCollins, 2003.

Nelson, Willie. *The Tao of Willie.* New York, NY: Gotham Books, 2007.

Ogilvy, David. *Ogilvy On Advertising.* New York, NY: Vintage Books, 1985.

Siebold, Steve. *177 Mental Toughness Secrets of the World Class.* Boynton Beach, FL: Gove-Seibold, 2005.

Trump, Donald, and Robert Kiyosaki. *Why We Want You To Be Rich.* Scottsdale, AZ: Rich Press, 2006.

Vitale, Joe. Spiritual Marketing. 1st Books Library, 2001.

Vitale, Joe. *The Attractor Factor.* Hoboken, NJ: John Wiley & Sons, 2005.

Vitale, Joe. *Hypnotic Writing.* Hoboken, NJ: John Wiley & Sons, 2006.

Vitale, Joe, and Bill Hibbler. *Meet and Grow Rich.* Hoboken, NJ: John Wiley & Sons, 2006.

Wind, Jerry, Colin Crook, and Robert Gunther. *The Power of Impossible Thinking.* Wharton School Publishing, Philadelphia, PA, 2006.

ONLINE RESOURCES

www.patobryan.com
www.patobryan.com/blog.htm
www.yourportableempire.com
www.portableempire.blogspot.com
www.patobryan.com/tools.htm
http://www.mythofpassiveincome.com
http://www.instantchange.com
http://www.pelmanismonline.com
http://www.listenandgrowrich.com
http://www.psychicdemand.com
www.milagroresearchinstitute.com/ebookproblemsolver.htm
http://www.milagroresearchinstitute.com/hyp.htm
http://www.influence101.com

THE PORTABLE EMPIRE
IN SEVEN STEPS

1. Choose your niche.
2. Identify a pressing problem in your niche.
3. Create a solution you can give away. Set up a squeeze page to exchange names and e-mail addresses in return for your solution.
4. Contact large list owners and arrange for them to give your freebie away. This will build your list and create relationships with future joint-venture partners.
5. Find more problems and create more solutions. Sell them to your list, and offer them to your JV partners to sell to their lists.
6. Continue building relationships with your subscribers and your JV partners.
7. Repeat to build multiple streams of passive income.

YOUR PORTABLE EMPIRE ONLINE

Now that you've read the book, you're ready to take advantage of *Your Portable Empire* online.

At www.yourportableempire.com, there is a web site with videos from all the Unseminars, audio interviews, and training with industry experts, online courses in copywriting, list building, product creation, and much, much more.

INDEX